SpringerBriefs in Geography

SpringerBriefs in Geography presents concise summaries of cutting-edge research and practical applications across the fields of physical, environmental and human geography. It publishes compact refereed monographs under the editorial supervision of an international advisory board with the aim to publish 8 to 12 weeks after acceptance. Volumes are compact, 50 to 125 pages, with a clear focus. The series covers a range of content from professional to academic such as: timely reports of state-of-the art analytical techniques, bridges between new research results, snapshots of hot and/or emerging topics, elaborated thesis, literature reviews, and in-depth case studies.

The scope of the series spans the entire field of geography, with a view to significantly advance research. The character of the series is international and multidisciplinary and will include research areas such as: GIS/cartography, remote sensing, geographical education, geospatial analysis, techniques and modeling, landscape/regional and urban planning, economic geography, housing and the built environment, and quantitative geography. Volumes in this series may analyze past, present and/or future trends, as well as their determinants and consequences. Both solicited and unsolicited manuscripts are considered for publication in this series.

SpringerBriefs in Geography will be of interest to a wide range of individuals with interests in physical, environmental and human geography as well as for researchers from allied disciplines.

More information about this series at https://link.springer.com/bookseries/10050

Thanh Phan · Daniela Damian
Editors

Smart Cities in Asia

Regulations, Problems, and Development

Springer

Editors
Thanh Phan
Faculty of Engineering
University of Victoria
Victoria, BC, Canada

Daniela Damian
Faculty of Engineering
University of Victoria
Victoria, BC, Canada

ISSN 2211-4165   ISSN 2211-4173   (electronic)
SpringerBriefs in Geography
ISBN 978-981-19-1700-4   ISBN 978-981-19-1701-1   (eBook)
https://doi.org/10.1007/978-981-19-1701-1

This Springer imprint is published by the registered company Springer Nature Singapore Pte Ltd.
The registered company address is: 152 Beach Road, #21-01/04 Gateway East, Singapore 189721, Singapore

Acknowledgements

We would like to send our sincere thanks to Prof. Victor V. Ramraj, Director of the Centre for Asia-Pacific Initiatives, University of Victoria; the Canadian Queen Elizabeth II Diamond Jubilee Scholarships-Advanced Scholars program and the Natural Sciences and Engineering Research Council of Canada for sponsoring our book project.

We are also grateful to Madeline Walker for assisting us with editing this book.

Finally, we would like to thank Robyn Fila and Katie Dey at the Centre for Asia-Pacific Initiatives, University of Victoria, for their tireless support.

Contents

Contents

Contributors

Hoa Chu Deputy Director General, Institute of Legal Studies, Ministry of Justice, Hanoi, Vietnam

B. Courtney Doagoo Centre for Law, Technology, and Society, University of Ottawa, Ottawa, Canada

Daniela Damian Faculty of Engineering, University of Victoria, Victoria, BC, Canada

Minh Son Ha Department Deputy, Academy of Finance, Hanoi, Vietnam

Ze Shi Li Faculty of Engineering, University of Victoria, Victoria, BC, Canada

Melinda Martinus ISEAS—Yusof Ishak Institute, Singapore, Singapore

Bryan Mercurio Faculty of Law, The Chinese University of Hong Kong, Shatin, New Territories, Hong Kong

Nguyen Thi Bich Ngoc Academy of Policy and Development, Hanoi, Vietnam

Thuy Linh Nguyen Academy of Finance, Hanoi, Vietnam

Thanh Phan Faculty of Engineering, University of Victoria, Victoria, BC, Canada

Visakha Phusamruat Graduate School of Law, National Institute of Development Administration, Bangkok, Thailand

Nguyen Van Cuong General Director, Institute of Legal Studies, Ministry of Justice of Vietnam, Hanoi, Vietnam

Colin Werner Faculty of Engineering, University of Victoria, Victoria, BC, Canada

Ronald Ker-Wei Yu Faculty of Law, The Chinese University of Hong Kong, Shatin, Hong Kong

Chapter 1
Introduction to Smart Cities in Asia: Regulations, Problems, and Development

Daniela Damian and Thanh Phan

Abstract Asia Pacific, which makes up 60% of the world's population, is emerging as a dynamic region in the world in terms of economic and technological growth. It is no surprise that Asian cities are also recognized as leaders in designing smart cities that harness digital information to improve operational efficiency. This chapter provides an overview of the subjects and jurisdictions that this book will cover, outlining its structure as well as the flow of the discussion. This book aims to provide audiences with an overview of smart cities in Asia from different perspectives. While the topic of Smart Cities in Asia: Regulations, Problems, and Development does not address all concerns and questions about smart cities in Asia, the discussions outline regulatory frameworks of some countries, addresses certain problems, and projects the development of smart cities in the region. The book also establishes a network of scholars and practitioners who are interested in researching smart cities. The editors and authors welcome all comments, suggestions, and initiatives promoting scholarship in this area.

Asia Pacific, which makes up 60% of the world's population, is emerging as a dynamic region in the world in terms of economic and technological growth (UNFPA, nd). Some countries in the region are leading performers in information and communication technology (ICT) indicators (UN ESCAP 2016). Also, East and North-East Asian countries contribute three-quarters of fixed broadband subscriptions in Asia (UN ESCAP 2016, p. 9).

It is no surprise that Asian cities are also recognized as leaders in designing smart cities that harness digital information to improve operational efficiency, and this book attempts to provide an introduction to some of the context, challenges

D. Damian · T. Phan (✉)
Faculty of Engineering, University of Victoria, 3800 Finnerty Road (Ring Road), Victoria, BC V8P 5C2, Canada
e-mail: thanhpc@uvic.ca

D. Damian
e-mail: danielad@uvic.ca

© The Author(s) 2022
T. Phan and D. Damian (eds.), *Smart Cities in Asia*, SpringerBriefs in Geography,
https://doi.org/10.1007/978-981-19-1701-1_1

and developments around smart cities in a number of countries in the region. Singapore, for example, is a city that consistently is ranked as 'one of the smartest cities' around, with a unique approach to centrally housing massive amounts of information collected from its citizens with the government instead of with an individual company. Other countries, such as Indonesia, Thailand and Vietnam or Korea, have developed smart cities at different levels and overcame challenges related to creating smart cities in traditional urban settings. Vietnam, for example, applied the smart city concept to governing a historical center in an ancient capital while Thailand is building a smart tourist city on an island.

1.1 Smart Cities: An Overview and General Issues

The concept of smart cities is not new, although it seems like a modern urbanism and sustainability-driven trend. The use of information technology and data for more efficient cities governance has become promising as early as 1970 when Los Angeles became known for its first urban big data project that used computer databases, cluster analysis, and infrared aerial photography to "gather data, produce reports on neighborhood demographics and housing quality, and help direct resources to ward off blight and tackle poverty" (Vallianatos 2015). Arguably the first smart city was Amsterdam in 1994 when it created a virtual digital city to promote Internet usage; the trend solidified in the 2000s with large corporations such as IBM and Cisco invested significantly in research and development of projects that used sensors, networks and analytics to help cities run more efficiently (Woetzel et al. 2021). Continued government and industry investment span off a growing number of smart cities initiatives in Japan (2010), Barcelona (2011), China (2013), and later other cities in Europe, Singapore and Vietnam, just to name a few.

As cities got smarter, the vision is that they are becoming more livable and more responsive as a result of leveraging technologies in urban environments. The last decade has seen an important shift from smart technologies being regarded as tools to improve efficiency to feasible enablers of a better quality of life. Technology and data used purposefully have become a powerful mechanism to make better decisions for a more livable future and sustainability has emerged as an aim of smart cities, as important as resource efficiency and governance (Woetzel et al. 2021). With the help of the Internet of Things (IoT) Technology to collect and analyze large, heterogenous amounts of data, sustainable smart cities are today's vision in bridging the gap between sustainability targets and urban development strategies. Rankings of most sustainable smart cities being topped by many European cities but also Asian cities like Singapore (Woetzel et al. 2021). While smart cities are now touted as imperative for a sustainable future, the approach is not without challenges: working with existing infrastructures in traditional cities when applying new technologies may be costly and unsuitable for cities with a long history, as described in some chapters in this book.

This book provides a discussion of the opportunities, developments and some of the challenges specific to smart cities in Asia. It starts in Chap. 2 with an overview and some definitions of smart cities, alongside perspectives from scholars and practitioners on problems with these cities from both legal and technical perspectives. Chapter 2 introduces a framework to conceptualize a few common topics related to smart city governance. Doagoo reviews the concept of smart cities discussed by scholars and international institutions such as the UN Economist Network, the UN Sustainable Development Goals, and the World Economic Forum 2019. The chapter also highlights some smart city initiatives in the world, sketches an overview of the smart city movements in Asian countries, and analyzes the various mechanics and concepts of smart cities to demonstrate that smart cities are not a one-size-fits-all approach. Finally, the author illustrates several common concerns and challenges relating to smart city governance, which include privacy, security, and public–private partnerships.

The concept of smart cities heavily relies on collecting large amounts of citizens' data and, as several chapters in the book highlight, can raise concerns as to what data is being used for. Because the processing of big data is an essential element as much as is the technological innovation in smart cities, the protection of privacy and personal data becomes pivotal to the sustainability and success of smart cities. While the internet and advanced technologies can help to optimize governance, they can also make people prone to cyberattacks. Chapter 3 starts this discussion by examining the ongoing challenges and solutions of managing data privacy for smart cities where data is collected from countless sensors and devices. By focusing on the technical aspects of data privacy, the authors show that while smart cities provide new business opportunities for software organizations to process, manage, utilize, examine, and generate data, they also create many privacy challenges. These challenges include obtaining a shared understanding of privacy and achieving compliance with privacy regulations. Li and Werner recognize that while smart cities support people's ability to make rational and prudent decisions based on real data, the privacy of that data should not be overlooked.

1.2 Legal Frameworks and Problems with Smart Cities in Asia: A Country Analysis

The following chapters focus the discussion of issues around privacy protection in specific regions, countries, and cities, using selected industries or case studies of smart city projects to illustrate benefits and challenges. In Chap. 4, Martinus explores the privacy concern of smart cities in the context of the COVID-19 pandemic in three active members of the Association of Southeast Asian Nations: Singapore, Malaysia, and Indonesia. The discussion starts with the concern of citizens, experts, and policymakers in the region about smart cities' data protection and security. Smart technologies, such as big data, artificial intelligence, and the Internet of

Things, are perceived as enablers for cities to control air pollution, reduce traffic, streamline public services, and make energy use more efficient. Experts, however, underline that personal and behavioral data collected by smart technologies have not been adequately protected, thus bringing significant risk to individual privacy. The COVID-19 pandemic has also further intensified the dialogue to address privacy concerns in the digital sphere. Drawing from the experience of COVID-19 tracing applications in Singapore, Malaysia, and Indonesia, the author finds that despite concerns about technical issues and accessibility, the practice of surveillance and the effectiveness of such technology adoption to fight COVID-19 remain in debate. The dialogue on data protection in the digital sphere has become more complex as there are contesting interests between the need to ensure public safety and the need to protect individual privacy.

Chapter 5 continues the thread of data and privacy in smart cities by discussing the need for a coherent policy on cross-border data flows to make the city of Hong Kong smart. Yu and Mercurio observe that to remain relevant and competitive, a smart city must rely on external data not only for short-term commercial needs, such as international payment transactions, but also for long-term innovation, content creation, product development, business viability, and support and updates for smart devices and vehicles. This requirement concurrently involves legal issues connected with privacy, trade, e-commerce, finance and cybersecurity, and intellectual property, which, in turn, is further complicated by the need to protect data, enforce laws, and access tools for the creation of new content or innovations. This chapter takes Hong Kong as a case study to examine the conflicting legal and other issues facing smart cities, including how to provide access to tools and data to enable the creation of apps, content, or products and adapt products for local and global needs; how to encourage use and deployment of data-dependent systems such as artificial intelligence; and how to allow companies to fulfill obligations to provide customer support, enable commercial transactions, or enable the flow of digital currencies. The authors advocate for the establishment of a coordinated framework and policy for managing cross-border data flows with respect to the governance of smart cities.

Moving to Thailand, Chap. 6 focuses on a specific smart city project in the tourist island of Phuket to highlight privacy and personal data-related issues arising from the development of smart cities. Based on recent smart city campaigns in Phuket involving closed-circuit television installation and digitally-tracking wristbands, Phusamruat finds that local actors' privacy perceptions and data processing practices substantially deviate from the privacy views and practices required by the Thai *Personal Data Protection Act*. This deviation may result in a lack of implementation of the *Act* or force inevitable changes to local community life to meet a new legal standard. The global–local tension between norms brought by visitors from various cultural backgrounds and the local tradition makes finding common ground far more difficult. This case demonstrates the limitations of current legal approaches to embracing diverse societal views and interests, while also paving a new way to understand privacy in smart cities and integrate this knowledge into their universal design.

Smart Cities require new strategies and regulatory frameworks to account for the renewed relationship between technology, government and society. The challenge is in establishing legal mechanisms that control the potential harm from technological advances and new services while enabling innovation (Gasiola 2022). Chapters 7 and 8 provide an overview of the legal framework for smart cities in Vietnam in recent years and the driving forces behind this evolution.

In Chap. 7, Nguyen (Cuong) highlights that the Vietnamese legal framework for smart city projects is still in an early stage of development with room for improvement, especially in the areas of legal rules for ICT application, urban governance of infrastructure, construction and engineering laws, intellectual property rights, and protection of personal data. This chapter shows that the promotion of smart city projects requires a huge effort from both central and local governments. The author believes that some local governments are active and interested in experimenting with smart city projects, but the lack of a sound legal framework could be a hindrance for realizing this ambition. This chapter also suggests that the central government should play a bigger role in constructing a legal framework that is more favorable to the implementation of smart city projects in local governments.

Further, Chu in Chap. 8 continues the discussion about the legal framework of Vietnam with a focus on personal data protection. Similar to other jurisdictions including Indonesia, Malaysia, Singapore, and Thailand, Vietnam has been revising its legal framework to address the need for personal data protection. The development of smart cities in Vietnam raises concerns among city residents about transparency in data collection and how to ensure that such data is not misused, disclosed, leaked, or exploited for the wrong purposes. This chapter reviews the Vietnamese legal framework for data protection to highlight that data protection law in Vietnam should be reformed for the development of smart cities.

Chapter 9 switches to the financial and banking aspect of smart cities in Vietnam. In cities where payments are expected to be digital, banking plays an important role. This chapter first reviews the literature on digital transformation in the banking sectors and the current commercial banks' digital transformation landscape in Vietnam. It provides examples of some local commercial banks to show that digital banking should be considered an integral part of smart cities. Ha and Nguyen (Linh) also analyze the challenges facing Vietnamese banks in their digitalization process to become smarter banks and puts forward some recommendations about how to leverage this process in the Vietnamese banking system. The authors assert that digital transformation is key to the banking industry creating value for the customer and keeping pace with innovation in smart cities where people expect real-time instant gratification.

Chapter 10 closes the discussion about smart cities in Vietnam by examining a case of the Intelligent Operations Center (IOC) in Thua Thien Hue province and analyzing its smart city implementation inside a historical and cultural city. The IOC, which was designed and implemented to lay a sound foundation for smart city technologies, helps the local government supervise and control citizens' social activities and predict social trends. The IOC also encourages the participation of citizens in managing the city. Nguyen (Ngoc) believes that the future of urban tourism belongs to smart cities and makes several recommendations to boost tourism and increase the participation of inhabitants in co-creating more value for the province in the smart city project.

1.3   Final Notes

This book aims to provide audiences with an overview of smart cities in Asia from different perspectives. While the topic of Smart Cities in Asia: Regulations, Problems, and Development does not address all concerns and questions about smart cities in Asia, the discussions outline regulatory frameworks of some countries, addresses certain problems, and projects the development of smart cities in the region. The book also establishes a network of scholars and practitioners who are interested in researching smart cities. The editors and authors welcome all comments, suggestions, and initiatives promoting scholarship in this area.

References

Gasiola GG (2022) Smart cities through smart regulation. Available at https://technologyandsociety. org/smart-cities-through-smart-regulation/. Accessed 5 Jan 2022

Hamza M (2021) These are the top 20 sustainable smart cities in the world. Available at https://www. disruptive-technologies.com/blog/the-top-20-sustainable-smart-cities-in-the-world. Accessed 12 Nov 2021

United Nations Population Fund Asia and the Pacific (UNFPA) (nd) Population trend. Available via UNFPA. https://asiapacific.unfpa.org/en/node/15207#:~:text=The%20Asia%20and%20the%20Pacific,Developing%20States%20in%20the%20Pacific. Accessed 29 July 2021

United Nations Economic and Social Commission for Asia and Pacific (UN ESCAP) (2016) State of ICT in Asia and the Pacific 2016: uncovering the widening broadband divide. Available via UN ESCAP. https://wedocs.unep.org/bitstream/handle/20.500.11822/8762/-State_of_ICT_in_ Asia_and_the_Pacific_Uncovering_the_widening_broadband_divide-2016State_of_ICT_in_ Asia_and_the_Pacific_2016.pdf.pdf?sequence=2&amp%3BisAllowed. Accessed 29 July 2021

Vallianatos M (2015) How LA used big data to build a smart city in the 1970s. Available at https://giz modo.com/uncovering-the-early-history-of-big-data-in-1974-los-an-1712551686. Accessed 15 Dec 2021

Woetzel J et al (2021) Smart cities: digital solutions for a more livable future. Available via McKinsey Global Institute. https://www.mckinsey.com/business-functions/operations/our-insights/smart-cities-digital-solutions-for-a-more-livable-future. Accessed 5 Dec 2021

Chapter 2
Smart Cities in Asia: An Introductory Note

B. Courtney Doagoo

Abstract This chapter provides a framework to conceptualize a few common topics related to smart city governance. It provides a high-level overview of smart cities movement in Asian countries, followed by the various mechanics and concepts of smart cities to demonstrate that there is no one-size-fits-all approach to create smart cities. It will then highlight several common concerns and challenges relating to smart city governance, which include privacy, security, and public–private partnerships.

2.1 Introduction

According to the World Bank, cities are home to roughly 55% of the world's population and account for more than 80% of its Gross Domestic Product (2020). It is projected that by 2030, about "752 million people will live in cities with at least 10 million inhabitants" (United Nations 2017, p. 3). Cities are therefore not only of central importance to the economy, but also have a critical impact on the environmental, political, and social lives of the individuals who inhabit them (World Bank 2020). Realizing the potential to improve people's lives along these axes, governments around the world have, for the last couple of decades, been looking to leverage various "smart city" initiatives to meet these goals. (IMD World Competitiveness 2020; People's Republic of China, nd).

Smart city initiatives are diverse and span across various industries. These initiatives can include opportunities to increase food security with urban community farming. Cities can target climate change through the implementation of smart mobility and smart grids, expansion of green spaces, and through the creation of 15-min city neighbourhoods. Smart city initiatives can also aim to increase access to services for citizens and civic participation (UN Economist Network 2020, pp. 12, 89). In addition to helping municipalities, provinces, and states benefit citizens, it has been suggested that smart cities can help countries work toward achieving the UN Sustainable Development Goals (SDGs) (Alisjahbana 2019). Smart cities have been

B. Courtney Doagoo (✉)
Centre for Law, Technology, and Society, University of Ottawa, Ottawa, Canada
e-mail: bdoag019@uottawa.ca

© The Author(s) 2022
T. Phan and D. Damian (eds.), *Smart Cities in Asia*, SpringerBriefs in Geography,
https://doi.org/10.1007/978-981-19-1701-1_2

identified as an opportunity to work toward attaining SDG 11, making "cities and human settlements inclusive, safe, resilient and sustainable" (IISD 2018) in addition to contributing to other SDGs.[1]

Smart city governance is a vast topic that encompasses numerous facets and elements. Given that in many cases, technology has been seen as the main enabler of smart city development, policymakers have been grappling with issues around governance within this environment (UN Report 2020, p. 89). While there are practical reasons for governments and citizens to encourage the development of smart cities, there are also regulatory, legal, policy, and ethical challenges that may limit these benefits or prevent them from being realized at all. (World Economic Forum 2020).[2] Recognizing the opportunities to leverage smart city initiatives, stakeholders have been keen to help smart cities realize their fullest potential while navigating these challenges (World Economic Forum 2019).[3] One such initiative is the G20 Global Smart Cities Alliance, which aims to "lead a new global effort to establish universal norms and guidelines for implementation of smart city technology" and to create a roadmap for cities to leverage policy and regulatory toolboxes for smart cities (World Economic Forum 2019).

It is difficult to know how many smart cities currently exist or are in development, as there are initiatives stemming across all continents (IMDWCC 2020). The earliest examples of smart cities have been said to include those in Europe, including Amsterdam and Barcelona. However, there has also been an increase in the growth and planning of smart cities in Asia. The key focus of this special series is smart cities in Asian countries, and while specific examples will be discussed throughout, many of the concepts, contentions, and challenges are universal and can apply to smart city initiatives across the world.

Given the vastness of this topic, this introductory note will provide an overview of the importance, approaches, and governance challenges associated with smart cities for the purpose of setting the stage for the chapters that follow. It is meant to provide a framework to conceptualize some of the issues and topics related to smart cities' governance. Part 2 provides a brief overview of the uptake of smart cities across Asian countries. Part 3 describes the various approaches in defining smart cities, developing them, and qualifying them to demonstrate that development and governance are not a one-size-fits-all approach (van Eerd 2020). Part 4 will

---

[1] The 2015 Resolution *A/RES/70/1 Transforming Our World: The 2030 Agenda for Sustainable Development* was adopted by the General Assembly with the aim of motivating member states to work together to achieve common goals towards a path of sustainable growth. The three underlying dimensions of the 17 goals are economic, social, and environmental. See https://www.un.org/ga/search/view_doc.asp?symbol=A/RES/70/1&Lang=E.

[2] In order to address the regulatory and policy framework, a roadmap is being developed to help participant cities navigate issues including "privacy protection, better broadband coverage, accountability for cyber security, increased openness of city data, and better accessibility to digital city services for disabled and elderly people".

[3] For example, in 2019, the World Economic Forum announced that it was going to lead the G20 Smart Cities Alliance on Technology.

then illustrate several common considerations and challenges relating to smart city governance, which include privacy, security, and public–private partnerships.

2.2 Adoption of Smart Cities: Focus on Asia

Smart cities play a significant role in Asia, as urbanization continues to increase rapidly. According to UN Habitat's *World Cities Report 2020*, it is estimated that, "[n]inety-six per cent of urban growth will occur in the less developed regions of East Asia, South Asia and Africa with three countries—India, China and Nigeria—accounting for 35 per cent of the total increase in global urban population from 2018 to 2050" (2020, p. 11). It is expected that during this time, India and China will increase by 416 and 255 million people respectively (UN Habitat 2020, p. 11) and that in China, there will be "221 cities with more than 1 million inhabitants" by 2025 (van Eerd 2020, p. 14).

Based on this anticipated increase and growth, it is unsurprising that smart cities are being embraced as a strategic opportunity for countries in this region. (Ludher et al. 2018).[4] New cities in China, India, and Korea are already being developed with networks that "interweave electricity, water, waste and gas systems," enhancing data generation and collection, which in turn helps monitor resources (OECD 2020a, b, p. 14). In 2020 it was revealed that there were over 500 smart cities being developed in China alone (Chandran 2020).

The Organisation for Economic Coordination and Development (OECD) reported that countries across Asia have developed their own "smart city strategy" (van Eerd 2020, p. 14). This is important to note, because it has been suggested that until now, much of the literature and research about smart city initiatives have been conducted through the lens of Western narratives, where there is greater participation by citizens and local governments. In the context of Asia, national governments play an important role and can often be seen as "the main actor, actively promoting and planning smart cities in many cases" (Joo and Tan 2020, p. 6). This can be seen in several jurisdictions such as in China (People's Republic of China 2016), Korea (Hwang 2020, p. 86), and Japan (Yarime 2020).

In the context of emerging Asian cities (Matsumoto et al. 2019, p. 4),[5] reportedly six out of 12 countries, including China, Singapore, and Thailand, have a national level smart city strategy (Matsumoto et al. 2019, p. 4). While engagement at the national level is positive as it signals commitment, collaboration and partnerships with regional and local governments is not always clear (Matsumoto et al. 2019, p. 8). This lack of clarity can lead to uncertainty in issues of governance and application.

---

[4] For example, recognizing the opportunities for collaboration, the Association of Southeast Asian Nations established their Smart Cities Network (ASCN) in 2018 and developed a smart city framework to help "sustainable urbanisation" to improve lives.

[5] This includes Southeast Asia, China, and India.

The following two sections will describe some of the common challenges related to developing, defining, and governing smart cities.

2.3   What Are Smart Cities? Defining Features

Defining smart cities is a useful exercise as it provides a starting point to conceptualize the various parameters of the term and to measure success. Despite smart cities being a widely used concept,[6] "smart" or "intelligent" cities have been defined in many ways. As highlighted by the United Nations Economic and Social Council in 2016, "[t]here is no standardized commonly accepted definition or set of terminologies for a smart city" (United Nations Economic and Social Council 2016, p. 3).

In 2020, the OECD defined smart cities as "initiatives or approaches that effectively leverage digitalisation to boost citizen well-being and deliver more efficient, sustainable and inclusive urban services and environments as part of a collaborative, multi-stakeholder process" ("Smart cities and inclusive growth" 2020, p. 8). Prior to this definition, in 2016 the International Telecommunications Union (ITU) and the United Nations Economic Commission for Europe (UNECE) developed a definition that highlighted similar themes: "[a] smart sustainable city is an innovative city that uses ICTs and other means to improve quality of life, efficiency of urban operation and services, and competitiveness, while ensuring that it meets the needs of present and future generations with respect to economic, social, environmental as well as cultural aspects" (2015, p. 3); United Nations Economic and Social Council (2016, p. 3).

In addition to these definitions, there are various qualifiers or "conceptual cousins" that have been used in the literature to further distinguish the goals or ambitions related to smart cities (Nam and Pardo 2011, p. 282). For example, smart cities have been qualified as "sustainable" (UNECE 2021) "ethical," (Global Smart Cities Alliance 2021) or "people-centered" (UN Habitat 2021) and can also be qualified as "digital," "intelligent," or "humane" cities (Nam and Pardo 2011, p. 284). Nam and Pardo categorize these concepts into three main dimensions of *technology, people, and institutions*"–noting that they are all "core factors" and "key conceptual components" of smart cities (2011, pp. 284–285). These factors seem to exist in all smart cities in varying degrees, depending on the city (Nam and Pardo 2011, pp. 286–287). The general goals of smart cities are efficiency, inclusivity, and economic and sustainable growth, with a focus on helping improve the quality and well-being

---

[6] For example, the report of the United Nations Economic and Social Council, "The UNECE-ITU Smart Sustainable Cities Indicators" Committee on Housing and Land Management Seventy-Sixth session 2015 ECE/HBP/2015/4 at 2 stated that as far back as 2012, the UNECE Committee on Housing and Land Management had identified "sustainable smart cities" as one of its priorities.

of its inhabitants' lives (UN Report 2020, p. 12). Two of the three factors, technology and institutional, will be highlighted briefly as they are directly related to the considerations discussed in the following section (Nam and Pardo 2011, p. 285).[7]

Technology can be seen as an enabler of the outcomes that smart city initiatives attempt to achieve. (Fleming 2020).[8] Smart city enabling technologies rely on the collection and use of data from numerous devices, Internet of Things (IoT), and sensors. Additionally, there is an ever-growing array of technologies that may greatly contribute to this environment–these include artificial intelligence (European Commission 2020), 5G networks (Huang 2021), blockchain (Hori 2021), and quantum computing technologies. (Shipilov 2019). These technologies are often developed and operated by private sector third party organizations.[9]

Various technologies can be implemented to enhance access to government services (e.g., digital identification, health) (Thales Group 2020), improve efficiencies (e.g., electricity, water management, traffic), help reduce impact on the environment (Carter and Boukerche 2020), and provide accessibility to transportation systems by reducing traffic and encouraging alternative mobility (OECD 2020a). There are several categories of smart city technologies, including "transportation," "water and electricity," "environmental monitoring," and "infrastructure and architecture" (Landry et al. 2018).

Smart cities rely on strategic vision and governance, in other words, the institutional factor. (Nam and Pardo 2011, pp. 286–287) As Nam and Pardo describe it, this factor considers how various communities and actors align to design and develop their smart city ambitions, and governance (2011, pp. 286–287). Smart cities can emerge in various ways. Conceptually, they can be top-down, bottom-up, or mixed. Top-down cities are those that are heavily planned and controlled. The vision of this smart city is one where everything is connected and managed through the "control room" (Breuer et al. 2014, p. 156). The top-down city is built from the ground up with all things designed and planned (Breuer et al. 2014, p. 156; Centre for Smart Cities, nd), where the emphasis is on driving and enhancing efficiencies and having a city run like clockwork. The bottom-up city relies on citizen engagement (Breuer et al. 2014, p. 157). Organic engagement and participation by individuals, local businesses, and communities are key. There are also variations of mixed initiatives, layers, and elements of smart cities that don't necessarily fall under either category (Capdevila and Zarlenga 2015).

The institutional dimension also covers public–private–people partnerships between one or several levels of government, the private sector, and individuals (Nam and Pardo 2011, pp. 286–287). Partnerships can contribute to the challenges that cities face when trying to adopt new "processes, practices and approaches"

---

[7] Finally, the *human* or people factor, perhaps the most important, centers on improving the lives of those who inhabit the smart city. As Nam and Pardo suggest, "[s]ocial infrastructure (intellectual capital and social capital) is indispensable endowment to smart cities".

[8] It is important to note that there are also low or non-technological solutions that can contribute to facilitating these outcomes; however, the risks associated with these will not be covered in this overview.

[9] More discussion about private–public partnerships below.

(OECD "Enhancing the contribution of smart cities" 2019, p. 21). Leveraging the private sector, for example, could be extremely beneficial for service delivery and access. The role or governance of partnerships will be discussed in the next section.

2.4 Smart City Technology Governance: Highlighting Challenges

The last decade has brought a significant shift in the way policymakers have been grappling with smart city governance. Organizations and policymakers have recognized and acknowledged the fact that emerging technology and its potential impacts have outpaced the regulatory frameworks that exist to protect individuals who interact with these technologies. This awareness was heightened as data—the foundational requirement for many technology-based smart city solutions—was declared the "new oil" in 2017 (Economist 2017).

Despite the various concepts or types of smart cities, for example, "sustainable" (UNECE 2021), "ethical" (Global Smart Cities Alliance, nd), or "people-centered" (UN Habitat, nd), there are cross-cutting challenges, especially as governments around the world are coming to terms with the far-reaching societal and ethical impacts of data and emerging technologies. In 2019, the World Economic Forum announced that it had been selected to lead a global forum to "establish universal norms and guidelines for implementation of smart city technology" in collaboration with the G20 presidency. At the time of writing this note, the "global policy roadmap" had developed "good practice" on several of the identified considerations, including information and communications technology (ICT) accessibility, open data, privacy impact assessment, and the cyber accountability model (World Economic Forum 2019). In the same year, 36 cities from around the world were selected as the inaugural participants in this program including selections in India, South Korea, Japan, and the Philippines (World Economic Forum 2020).

How these challenges are practically addressed will vary based on the jurisdiction and, as a result, the regulatory frameworks present within those jurisdictions. For example, in the context of data collection and use, what might be deemed appropriate based on the regulatory framework in one jurisdiction will be vastly different in another (e.g., the *General Data Protection Regulation*[10] versus other jurisdictions). For this reason, the examples provided in this section are general and are meant to illustrate the universal considerations associated with smart cities. Even where they do not breach laws or regulations within the jurisdiction they occur, the possible outcome, that is the potential harm or impact on an individual, remains the same.

---

[10] Regulation (EU) 2016/679 of the European Parliament and of the Council of 27 April 2016 on the protection of natural persons with regard to the processing of personal data and on the free movement of such data, and repealing Directive 95/46/EC.

2.4.1 Privacy

In the context of smart cities, technology-enabled solutions rely on the collection and use of vast amounts of data, including personal data, from numerous sources. These can include the collection and use of biometric, behavioral, and other types of information from IoT connected devices such as sensors, meters, and cellphones. How this data is used and for what purpose is an important question. As we rely more heavily on artificial intelligence and automation, there are additional risks of harm in some contexts.

Public trust is central to uptake and to civic participation. As pointed out by the OECD, in addition to considering governance issues related to competition and the economy, the "shift from an economy of infrastructure to an economy of applications will only work if data is perceived as being in safe hands" (OECD 2020b, p. 45). The TraceTogether contact tracing app, developed (Singapore Government Developer Portal 2021) and launched by the government of Singapore, while not a direct example of a smart city technology, received backlash as the government revealed that the information they confirmed would be collected for the purpose of contact tracing, could also be used in criminal and other inquiries (Illmer 2021). The public reaction prompted new legislation to be tabled in parliament (Yi-Ling and Abdul Rahman 2021).

The use of facial recognition and surveillance technology is also a legitimate concern as the extent and impact of the information being collected and used is often unknown to the individual. In 2019, TechCrunch revealed that a database containing data including "facial recognition scans on hundreds of people over several months" was accessed on a web browser that was not password secured (Whittaker 2021). The information revealed the movement of a subsection of individuals residing in a neighborhood including "where people went, when and for how long, allowing anyone with access to the data—including police—to build up a picture of a person's day-to-day life" (Whittaker 2021).While there may be regulatory implications for the ubiquitous collection and use of data in some jurisdictions, there are also interesting ethical considerations, including profiling.

Some jurisdictions are looking at creative opportunities to overcome concerns about privacy and consent The city of Aizuwakamatsu in Japan, adopted an "opt-in" approach for smartphone disaster alerts and various digital services in "mobility, education, healthcare, and energy consumption" which provides citizens with some level of control over the use of their data (Chandran 2021).

2.4.2 Security

Security is a particularly interesting aspect of smart cities because the potential vulnerabilities do not apply only to individuals, but also to infrastructures and services (Kitchin 2019; Muggah and Goodman 2019). For example, in 2018, it was reported that IBM and Threatcare identified 17 vulnerabilities in smart cities around the world, which would have impacted traffic light and flood warning systems (Ng 2018). There are a wide range of actors who might benefit from breaching or disrupting cities. These may include state actors, organized crime, terrorist groups, individuals, or businesses (CPAC 2019, p. 11). There is also the possibility of (information technology and IoT) systems being vulnerable to disasters (CPAC 2019, p. 11).

In 2021, the United Kingdom's National Cyber Security Centre issued guidance, suggesting that smart cities, due to the need to collect, process, and store sensitive data, could be "an attractive target for a range of threat actors" (Corera 2021; National Cyber Security Centre 2021). The Government of Canada also noted the potential threat to the safety of Canadians because of connected smart devices and smart cities (Communications Security Establishment 2020, p. 12). Additionally, it was reported that in the United States, "a quarter of local governments were facing attempted cyberattacks every hour" in 2016 (G20 Global Cities Alliance; Pandey et al. 2020).

The challenges with security stem from various issues. One of these issues is that given many cities have legacy systems intermixed with new applications, the level of security might not be standard across the board (Nussbaum 2016). Another security issue is the sheer number of sensors and connected devices gathering information for difference purposes. For example, a single neighborhood could collect data about energy, electricity and hydro, traffic, cars, front doors, and mobile devices. The implications of geographically concentrated information gathering can be far-reaching for individuals and systems (Nussbaum 2016).

2.4.3 Private–Public Partnership

Smart cities rely heavily on public–private partnerships (including partnerships with universities and non-governmental organizations) (McKinsey Global Institute 2019) across various industries, including telecommunications, energy, digital health, and agriculture. In 2019, the OECD highlighted the fact that the private sector has played a significant role as "advocate, investor and gamechanger in the use of technologies to define and address a range of problems in selected sectors; it is now confronted with the challenge of considering new forms of public–private collaborations to facilitate the uptake of these initiatives in the face of megatrends, regulatory change and infrastructure needs" (OECD 2019, p. 11).

In 2017, the World Economic Forum highlighted the benefits of private sector involvement in urban development and transformation, including the advantages of investment, innovation, management, and risk management (World Economic Forum 2017, p. 26) in the context of the UN New Urban Agenda, stating that, "a concise, focused, forward-looking and action-oriented plan … provides a new global strategy on urbanization for the next two decades" (World Economic Forum 2017, p. 6). There are numerous examples of public–private partnerships across smart cities in Asia. For example, Alibaba developed an intelligence system called ET City Brain and deployed it across 23 Asian cities (Alibaba Clouder 2019). ET City Brain has contributed to vast improvements in various areas. For example, in Hangzhou this program has assisted in traffic reduction, the purchase of parking passes, and vehicle licensing, and even checking into hotels (Alibaba Clouder 2019).

In 2019, Japan created a "Smart City Public–Private Partnership Platform" where over 100 cities and 300 companies have signed up to promote "knowledge exchange, business matching, and closer ties between public, private and academia" (Japan BrandVoice 2019). Furthermore, at the national level, Japan enacted a law in 2020 to "improve the collaboration between the public and private sectors for the digital transformation of cities" (Hirayama and Rama 2021), while at the local level, cities have been driving collaboration with the private sector to enhance digital transformation and data sharing (Hirayama and Rama 2021).

As stated by the OECD,

> shifting from a government-led approach to public–private collaboration is an important priority. Smart city projects can only be successful if they engage a variety of stakeholders, such as technology developers and service providers (who make technology); city developers (who add technology); city administrators (who use technology); residents and local companies (who purchase technology). (van Eerd 2020, p. 9)

Despite the benefits, important challenges can arise from these partnerships. These challenges relate to data governance and questions of "ownership" (Scassa 2020). They can also relate to privacy and security. Teresa Scassa highlights the complexity of smart city data governance given the various actors and sources,

> Public sector access to information and protection of privacy legislation provides some sort of framework for transparency and privacy when it comes to public sector data, but clearly such legislation is not well adapted to the diversity of smart cities data. While some data will be clearly owned and controlled by the municipality, other data will not be. Further the increasingly complex relationship between public and private sectors around input data and data analytics means that there will be a growing number of conflicts between rights of access and transparency on the one hand, and the protection of confidential commercial information on the other. (Scassa 2018)

As she points out, there can be important differences between the regulatory requirements and the objectives of the private and public sectors. These differences can result in an erosion of trust between the public and government efforts to encourage adoption and processes. The importance of partnerships cannot be overstated, as there are clear boundaries in the capacity of governments to fulfill the mandate of smart cities on their own.

2.5 Conclusion

Asian cities are poised to be impacted by high urban growth in upcoming decades. Given the potential density in urban areas, governments are looking ahead to develop smart cities to alleviate congestion and pollution, reduce the impact of climate change, and enhance civic engagement and mobility.

Smart cities do not follow a one-size-fits-all approach: no two smart cities are alike. They are a product of many considerations, including whether they are a result of a national or regional strategy, the objectives they are attempting to achieve, and the regulatory and social framework within which they operate. They are also the product of the degree to which levers of institutional, technology, and human factors are at play. Despite the differences between smart cities, they share several commonalities related to challenges and risks related to privacy, security, and public–private partnerships. In addition to questions of governance, public–private partnerships can play an important role in shaping the public's uptake of trust in the adoption and acceptance of smart city initiatives.

References

Alibaba Clouder (2019) City brain now in 23 cities in Asia. Available via Alibaba Cloud. https://www.alibabacloud.com/blog/city-brain-now-in-23-cities-in-asia_595479?spm=a2c65. 11461447.0.0.4b93185aJbxquz. Accessed 30 Aug 2021

Alisjahbana AS (2019) Smart cities hold the key to sustainable development. United Nations, Economic and Social Commission for Asia and the Pacific. Available via UN ESCAP. https://www.unescap.org/op-ed/smart-cities-hold-key-sustainable-development. Accessed 29 Aug 2021

Breuer J et al (2014) Beyond defining the smart city: meeting top-down and bottom-up approaches in the middle. In: Journal of land use, mobility and environment special issue eight international conference input: smart city—planning for energy, transportation and sustainability of the urban system, 2–4 June 2014

Capdevila I, Zarlenga MI (2015) Smart city of smart citizens? The Barcelona case. J Strat Manage 8(3):266. https://doi.org/10.1108/JSMA-03-2015-0030/full/html.

Carter L, Boukerche S (2020) Catalyzing private sector investment in climate-smart cities. Invest4Climate knowledge series. Available via World Bank https://documents1.worldbank.org/curated/en/179101596519553908/pdf/Catalyzing-Private-Sector-Investment-in-Climate-Smart-Cities.pdf. Accessed 30 Aug 2021

Centre for Cities (2014) What is a smart city: a concept lost in translation? Available via Centre for Cities. https://www.centreforcities.org/reader/smart-cities/what-is-a-smart-city/. Accessed 30 Aug 2021

Chandran R (2020) Tencent's 'smart city' seen as model for post-coronavirus China. Available via Thomson Reuters Foundation News. https://news.trust.org/item/20200624080235-95zxs as cited in Bacchi U (2020) 'I know your favourite drink': Chinese smart city to put AI in charge. Available via World Economic Forum https://www.orum.org/agenda/2020/12/china-ai-techno logy-city/. Accessed 30 Aug 2021

Chandran R (2021) How Japan's 'opt-in' smart city could change urban living. Available via World Economic Forum https://www.weforum.org/agenda/2021/03/japanese-smart-city-reside nts-privacy-protection-data/. Accessed 30 Aug 2021

Communications Security Establishment (2020) Canadian Centre for Cyber Security: National Cyber Threat Assessment 2020. Available via Communications Security Establishment https://cyber.gc.ca/sites/default/files/publications/ncta-2020-e-web.pdf

Corera G (2021) Spy bosses warn of cyber-attacks on smart cities. Available via BBC News. https://www.bbc.com/news/technology-57012725. Accessed 1 Sept 2021

Cybersecurity and Privacy Advisory Committee (CPAC) (2019) Smart and secure cities and communities challenge (SC3): a risk management approach to smart city cybersecurity and privacy. Available via CPAC. https://pages.nist.gov/GCTC/uploads/blueprints/2019_GCTC-SC3_Cybers ecurity_and_Privacy_Advisory_Committee_Guidebook_July_2019.pdf. Accessed 1 Sept 2021

Economist (2017) The world's most valuable resource is no longer oil, but data. Available via The Economist. https://www.economist.com/leaders/2017/05/06/the-worlds-most-valuable-resource-is-no-longer-oil-but-data. Accessed 1 Sept 2021

European Commission (2020) DIH webinar: artificial intelligence for smart cities. Available via European Commission. https://digital-strategy.ec.europa.eu/en/library/dih-webinar-artificial-intelligence-smart-cities. Accessed 1 Sept 2021

European Commission, Regulation (EU) (2016) 2016/679 of the European Parliament and of the Council of 27 April 2016 on the protection of natural persons with regard to the processing of personal data and on the free movement of such data, and repealing Directive 95/46/EC (General Data Protection Regulation)

Fleming A (2020) The case for …making low-tech 'dumb' cities instead of 'smart' ones. Available via The Guardian https://www.theguardian.com/cities/2020/jan/15/the-case-for-making-low-tech-dumb-cities-instead-of-smart-ones. Accessed 1 Sept 2021

Global Smart Cities Alliance (2021) Global policy roadmap. Available via G20 Global Smart Cities Alliances https://globalsmartcitiesalliance.org/?page_id=90. Accessed 1 Sept 2021

Hirayama Y, Rama R (2021) Japan's smart city initiatives will play key role in its digitisation and economic revival. Available via World Economic Forum https://www.weforum.org/agenda/2021/04/japan-smart-city-initiatives-digitisation-economic-revival-gtgs/. Accessed 30 Aug 2021

Hori S (2021) How blockchain can empower smart cities—and why interoperability will be crucial. Available via World Economic Forum https://www.weforum.org/agenda/2021/04/how-blockchain-can-empower-smart-cities-gtgs21/. Accessed 30 Aug 2021

Huang M (2021) Making smart cities: the power of hackathons brings together Rogers, UBC students, city of Kelowna, and Microsoft to advance 5G smart city applications. Available via Microsoft. https://www.microsoft.com/en-us/garage/blog/2021/05/making-smart-cities-the-power-of-hackathons/. Accessed 1 Sept 2021

Hwang J-S (2020) The evolution of smart city in South Korea: the smart city winter and the city-as-a-platform. In: Joo Y-M, Tan T-B (eds) Smart cities in Asia: governing development in the era of hyper-connectivity. Edward Elgar Publishing, Toronto

Illmer A (2021) Singapore reveals Covid privacy data available to police. Available via BBC News. https://www.bbc.com/news/world-asia-55541001. Accessed 1 Sept 2021

International Telecommunications Union (ITU) (2021) Goal 11. Cities. Available via ITU https://www.itu.int/en/sustainable-world/Pages/goal11.aspx. Accessed 1 Sept 2021

IMD World Competitiveness Center (IMDWCC), SCO Smart City Observatory and Singapore University of Technology and Design (2020) Smart city index 2020: a tool for action, an instrument for better living for all citizens. Available via IMD https://www.imd.org/smart-city-observatory/smart-city-index/. Accessed 29 Aug 2021

IISD SDG Knowledge Hub (2018) SDG 11: building the world's smart sustainable cities together. Available via IISD https://sdg.iisd.org/commentary/guest-articles/sdg-11-building-the-worlds-smart-sustainable-cities-together/. Accessed 1 Sept 2021

Japan BrandVoice (2019) Japan sparks new life in local communities with human-centric smart cities. Available via Forbes https://www.forbes.com/sites/japan/2019/12/23/japan-sparks-new-life-in-local-communities-with-human-centric-smart-cities/?sh=a6c59c34398e. Accessed 1 Sept 2021

Joo Y-M, Tan T-B (2020) Smart cities in Asia: an introduction. In Joo Y-M, Tan T-B (eds) Smart cities in Asia: governing development in the era of hyper-connectivity. Edward Elgar Publishing, Toronto

Kitchin R, Dodge M (2019) The (in)security of smart cities: vulnerabilities, risks, mitigation, and prevention. Available via Kitchin.org. https://kitchin.org/wp-content/uploads/2020/02/JUT-2019-Security-of-Smart-Cities.pdf. Accessed 6 Sept 2020

Landry J-N et al (2018) Open smart cities guide. Available via Samuelson-Glushko Canadian Internet Policy and Public Interest Clinic (CIPPIC). https://cippic.ca/en/Open_Smart_Cities. Accessed 6 Sept 2021

Ludher E et al (2018) ASEAN smart cities network. Available via Centre for Liveable Cities Singapore https://www.clc.gov.sg/docs/default-source/books/book-asean-smart-cities-net work.pdf. Accessed 30 Aug 2021

Matsumoto T et al (2019) Trends for smart city strategies in emerging Asia. Available via OECD Regional Development Working Papers 2019/10. https://www.oecd-ilibrary.org/urban-rural-and-regional-development/trends-for-smart-city-strategies-in-emerging-asia_4fcef080-en. Accessed 1 Sept 2021

McKinsey Global Institute (2019) How can the private and public sectors work together to create smart cities? Available via MGI https://www.mckinsey.com/business-functions/operations/our-insights/how-can-the-private-and-public-sectors-work-together-to-create-smart-cities. Accessed 1 Sept 2021

Muggah R, Goodman M (2019) Cities are easy prey for cybercriminals. Here's how they can fight back. Available via World Economic Forum https://www.weforum.org/agenda/2019/09/our-cities-are-increasingly-vulnerable-to-cyberattacks-heres-how-they-can-fight-back/. Accessed 1 Sept 2021

Nam T, Pardo PA (2011) Conceptualizing smart city with dimensions of technology, people, and institutions. In: Proceedings of the 12th Annual International Conference on Digital Government Research. University at Albany, June 2011. 282–291. https://doi.org/10.1145/2037556.2037602. Accessed 29 Aug 2021

National Cyber Security Centre (2021) Connected places cyber security principles. Available via United Kingdom Government https://www.ncsc.gov.uk/files/NCSC-Connected-Places-security-principles-May-2020.pdf. Accessed 1 Sept 2021

Ng A (2018) Smart cities around the world were exposed to simple hacks. Available via cnet. https://www.cnet.com/news/smart-cities-around-the-world-were-exposed-to-simple-hacks/. Accessed 1 Sept 2021

Nussbaum B (2016) Smart cities—the cyber security and privacy implications of ubiquitous urban computing. Available via Stanford Center for Internet and Society http://cyberlaw.stanford.edu/blog/2016/02/smart-cities-cyber-security-and-privacy-implications-ubiquitous-urban-com puting. Accessed 1 Sept 2021

Organisation for Economic Coordination and Development (2019) Enhancing the contribution of digitalisation to the smart cities of the future. Available via OECD https://www.oecd.org/cfe/reg ionaldevelopment/Smart-Cities-FINAL.pdf. Accessed 1 Sept 2021

Organisation for Economic Cooperation and Development (OECD) (2020a) Leveraging digital technology and data for human-centric smart cities: the case of smart mobility report for the G20 digital economy task force. Available via OECD International Transportation Forum. https://www.itf-oecd.org/sites/default/files/docs/data-human-centric-cities-mobility-g20.pdf. Accessed 29 Aug 2021

Organisation for Economic Cooperation and Development and Ministry of Land, Infrastructure and Transport, Korea (2020b) Smart cities and inclusive growth: building on the outcomes of the 1st OECD roundtable on smart cities and inclusive growth. Available via OECD https://www.oecd.org/cfe/cities/OECD_Policy_Paper_Smart_Cities_and_Inclusive_Growth.pdf. Accessed 29 Aug 2021

Pandey P et al (2020) Making smart cities cybersecure: ways to address distinct risks in an increasingly connected urban future. Available via Deloitte Center for Government Insights https://www2.deloitte.com/content/dam/Deloitte/de/Documents/risk/Report_mak ing_smart_cities_cyber_secure.pdf. Accessed 1 Sept 2021

People's Republic of China (nd) The 13th five-year plan for economic and social development of the People's Republic of China (2016–2020). Available via Government of the People's Republic of China https://en.ndrc.gov.cn/policies/202105/P020210527785800103339.pdf. Accessed 1 Sept 2021

Personal Information Protection and Electronic Documents Act (PIPEDA), SC 2000, c 5

Scassa T (2018) Smart cities data—governance challenges. Available via Teresa Scassa [blog]. https://www.teresascassa.ca/index.php?option=com_k2&view=item&id=285:smart-cit ies-data-governance-challenges&Itemid=80

Scassa T (2020) Designing data governance for data sharing: lessons from sidewalk Toronto. Available via Technology and Regulation 44. https://techreg.org/index.php/techreg/article/view/51. Accessed 1 Sept 2021

Shipilov A (2019) The real business case for quantum computing. Available via INSEAD. https://knowledge.insead.edu/blog/insead-blog/the-real-business-case-for-quantum-computing-10836. Accessed 1 Sept 2021

Singapore Government Developer Portal (2021) TradeTogether-community-drive contract tracing. Available via Singapore Government Developer Portal. https://www.developer.tech.gov.sg/tec hnologies/digital-solutions-to-address-covid-19/tracetogether. Accessed 1 Sept 2021

Thales Group (2020) Singapore: the world's smartest city. Available via Thales Group. https:// www.thalesgroup.com/en/worldwide-digital-identity-and-security/iot/magazine/singapore-wor lds-smartest-city. Accessed 1 Sept 2021

United Nations 2015 Resolution (2015) A/RES/70/1 transforming our world: the 2030 agenda for sustainable development. Available via United Nations. https://www.un.org/ga/search/view_doc. asp?symbol=A/RES/70/1&Lang=E

United Nations Economic Commission for Europe (2021) Sustainable smart cities. Available via UNECE. https://unece.org/housing/sustainable-smart-cities. Accessed 1 Sept 2021

United Nations Economic and Social Council (UNECE) (2015) The UNECE-ITU smart sustainable cities indicators. Committee on Housing and Land Management. Seventy-sixth session 2015 ECE/HBP/2015/4. Available via UNECE. https://unece.org/DAM/hlm/projects/SMART_ CITIES/ECE_HBP_2015_4.pdf. Accessed 30 Aug 2021

United Nations Economic and Social Council (UNECE) (2016) Smart cities and infrastructure: report of the Secretary General Commission on Science and Technology for Development. Nineteenth Session E/CN.16/2016/2 (May 9–13, 2016). Available via UNCTAD. https://unctad.org/ system/files/official-document/ecn162016d2_en.pdf. Accessed 30 Aug 2021

United Nations Economist Network (2020) Report of the UN economist network for the UN 75th anniversary: shaping the trends of our time. Available at UN. https://www.un.org/development/ desa/publications/wp-content/uploads/sites/10/2020/10/20-124-UNEN-75Report-Full-EN-REV ISED.pdf. Accessed 29 Aug 2021

United Nations Habitat (2020) World cities report 2020: the value of sustainable urbanization. Available via UN Habitat https://unhabitat.org/sites/default/files/2020/10/wcr_2020_report.pdf. Accessed 29 Aug 2021

United Nations Habitat (2021) People-centered smart cities. Available via UN Habitat https://unh abitat.org/programme/people-centered-smart-cities. Accessed 30 Aug 2021

United Nations, Population Division, World Urbanization Prospects 2018 (2017) The world's cities in 2018: data booklet. https://www.un.org/en/events/citiesday/assets/pdf/the_worlds_cities_in_ 2018_data_booklet.pdf. Accessed 29 Aug 2021

van Eerd R et al (2020) 2020 policy note on Asia: smart cities as engines for growth. Available via Organisation for Economic Coordination and Development. https://www.oecd.org/dev/EMnet-Asia-Policy-Note-2020.pdf. Accessed 6 Sept 2021

Whittaker Z (2021) Security lapse exposed a Chinese smart city surveillance system. Available via TechCrunch. https://techcrunch.com/2019/05/03/china-smart-city-exposed/. Accessed 30 Aug 2021

World Bank (2020) Urban development. https://www.worldbank.org/en/topic/urbandevelopment/ overview#:~:text=With%20more%20than%2080%25%20of,and%20new%20ideas%20to%20e merge. Accessed 29 Aug 2021

World Economic Forum Prepared in Collaboration with PwC (2017) Harnessing public-private cooperation to deliver the new urban agenda. Available via WEF. http://www3.weforum.org/ docs/WEF_Harnessing_Public-Private_Cooperation_to_Deliver_the_New_Urban_Agenda_ 2017.pdf. Accessed 30 Aug 2021

World Economic Forum (2019) World economic forum to lead G20 smart cities alliance on technology governance. Available via WEF https://www.weforum.org/press/2019/06/world-eco nomic-forum-to-lead-g20-smart-cities-alliance-on-technology-governance/. Accessed 30 Aug 2021

World Economic Forum (2020) In the face of extraordinary challenges, 36 pioneer cities chart a course towards a more ethical and responsible future. Available via WEF. https://www.weforum.org/press/2020/11/in-the-face-of-extraordinary-challenges-36-pio neer-cities-chart-a-course-towards-a-more-ethical-and-responsible-future. Accessed 29 Aug 2021

Yarime M (2020) Facilitating innovation for smart cities: the role of public policies in the case of Japan. In: Joo Y-M, Tan T-B (eds) Smart cities in Asia: governing development in the era of hyper-connectivity. Edward Elgar Publishing, Toronto

Yi-Ling T, Abdul Rahman MF (2021) Someone to watch over me: trusting surveillance in Singapore's 'smart nation'. Available via The Diplomat https://thediplomat.com/2021/01/someone-to-watch-over-me-trusting-surveillance-in-singapores-smart-nation/. Accessed 1 Sept 2021

Chapter 3
Ongoing Challenges and Solutions of Managing Data Privacy for Smart Cities

Ze Shi Li and Colin Werner

Abstract Smart cities represent the epitome of utilizing data sourced from sensors and devices in a city to make informed decisions. Facilitating the massive breadth of data are millions and billions of "smart" devices interconnected through high-speed telecommunication networks, so naturally software organizations began specializing in various parts of the smart city data spectrum. In a smart city, new business opportunities are created for software organizations to process, manage, utilize, examine, and generate data. While smart cities support the ability to make rational and prudent decisions based on real data, the privacy of the data cannot be overlooked. In particular, there are privacy challenges regarding the collection, analysis, and dissemination of data. More precisely, we recognize that there are a multitude of challenges facing software organizations, which include obtaining a shared understanding of privacy and achieving compliance with privacy regulations.

3.1 Introduction

Smart cities are increasingly receiving attention and praise as the future model of future living and working. Smart cities promise an improved quality of life and more informed decision-making, so it is no surprise that major headlines follow whenever a new smart city project is announced. Major cities around the world believe in the potential of smart cities and are buying in, hoping to become one of the premier and trailblazing cities that establish a leadership position in becoming a "smart" city (Earth.Org 2021).

According to McKinsey and Company (Woetzel et al. 2021), there are three layers of smartness that work together to produce an effective smart city, namely bottom, middle, and upper layer. The bottom layer consists of any device that has sensors

Z. S. Li (✉) · C. Werner
Faculty of Engineering, University of Victoria, 3800 Finnerty Road (Ring Road), Victoria, BC
V8P 5C2, Canada
e-mail: lize@uvic.ca

C. Werner
e-mail: colinwerner@uvic.ca

© The Author(s) 2022
T. Phan and D. Damian (eds.), *Smart Cities in Asia*, SpringerBriefs in Geography,
https://doi.org/10.1007/978-981-19-1701-1_3

and can interconnect with other devices via high-speed internet. Hence, any device that can collect data such as microwaves, traffic lights, digital doorbells, ovens, and buses are categorized as the bottom layer. The middle layer consists of applications that convert raw data collected from smartphones and sensors into metrics. These metrics are further analyzed into meaningful insights. Any software organization that develops or maintains software that aggregates and/or processes the data for analytical purposes is also part of the middle layer. After all, the focal point of the middle layer is deducing logical conclusions from the data collected in the bottom layer. Finally, the upper layer consists of organizations, municipal bodies, and the public as a whole. The first two layers set the groundwork to inform and help the third layer make rational decisions. For example, data about the capacity of buses would allow commuters to decide on the best route to take and avoid overcrowding or extended waits. Similarly, data about water consumption could help inform dwellers about their water usage and prompt them to repair broken or leaky pipes that unnecessarily waste water.

Ultimately, the crucial component to a successful smart city revolves around the robust integration of data and technology (Tuerk 2019), in particular, the linkage of data and technology to facilitate key decision-making. This linkage of data and technology creates new opportunities and benefits for software organizations, whether an organization creates sensors or devices to collect data or develops software that seeks to analyze metrics or data collected from individual devices. A new age of innovation is upon us, where an organization can specialize in aggregating and conducting large-scale comprehensive analysis on real-life data and produce useful results that are later used by other organizations. A significant range of business opportunities now exists for organizations that help process and understand the raw data.

Based on current levels of data and device interconnectivity, cities still have a long way to go before they reach the pinnacle of "smart" cities (Tuerk 2019). Yet, the battle for the top "smart" city is ever so fierce as cities around the globe engage in new infrastructure and technological projects often with the support of their national governments. Some of the more pronounced proposed smart city projects at one point included Hudson's Yards in New York, Sidewalk Labs in Toronto, and Xiong'an New Area near Beijing. Each project involves massive amounts of investment in people, property, and technology. For instance, the Hudson's Yards project was proclaimed as one of the most expensive private real estate projects in the history of the United States. Likewise, the Sidewalk Toronto project was supposed to develop one of the largest areas of underdeveloped urban lands in Canada and build a testbed neighbourhood for groundbreaking technologies. When completed, the proposed "neighbourhood" will have the highest levels of sustainability, economic opportunity, housing affordability, and new mobility.

Smart city projects are not without risks. Specifically, the Sidewalk Labs project was marred with controversy from its inception before ultimately terminating in 2020 due to economic uncertainty stemming from COVID-19. Critics of the project fiercely opposed the planned development due to the lack of transparency regarding data privacy and the potential for personal data infringement once the project is completed. Moreover, the project did not adequately disclose how or where data would be stored. While the project organizers assured Toronto residents that data would be anonymized before disclosing to the public, previous studies have shown that anonymized data can still be combined with other datasets to de-anonymize the protected data.

Ultimately, Sidewalk Toronto failed, but similar projects are in preparation or under development in other cities. The data privacy challenges highlighted by critics of the project represent a legitimate concern about smart cities. In this chapter, we discuss the difficulty of managing data privacy for software organizations that may develop software for processing, managing, or generating data. In particular, we describe the difficulty for software organizations in achieving a shared understanding of privacy and complying with privacy regulations.

3.2 Managing Privacy

As previously mentioned, the collection and analysis of data are critical to the success of a smart city. Correspondingly, the safeguarding and adequate handling of any private data are also vital to the privacy interests of the local population whose data is collected. Yet, when we take a deeper look at modern, agile organizations that develop software, we notice that they often have to make difficult trade-offs when dealing with software attributes, such as privacy. A previous study found that small, agile software organizations using continuous practices (i.e., a software development methodology emphasizing automation and rapid feedback that is ubiquitous in modern software developing organizations) manage software attributes, like privacy, via four main practices: (1) put a number on the attribute, (2) let someone else manage the attribute, (3) write your own tool to check the attribute, or (4) put the attribute in source control (Werner et al. 2021).

For the studied organizations, to deal with attributes of their software, the first step is assigning a number (i.e., metric) to the attribute. Assigning a metric to the privacy attribute may seem rudimentary or trivial; however, it is critical to reliably test whether the attribute was achieved or not. For example, a privacy attribute may prescribe that personal data may not stay on record for any longer than 90 days. Identifying the specifics regarding the legal limits for the data storage is at the crux of satisfying the privacy attribute. Imagine if the privacy attribute instead prescribed that "personal data may not stay on record for a lengthy period." In this scenario, a developer or team in charge of carrying out the privacy attribute would have the onerous task of trying to discern what means "lengthy period" means. The use of "lengthy" becomes a precarious problem, as either 30 or 180 days could be considered lengthy depending on who is asked to make the determination. Moreover, such ambiguous privacy attributes make communication to customers and users a difficult problem for the software organization. As previously noted, a primary concern on the part of smart city residents involves the handling of the privacy of the data collected within the boundaries of the smart city. Hence, transparency and communication of how privacy is handled are paramount to satisfy the concerns of residents. Providing clear measurements regarding how or what data is collected is more convincing than ambiguous alternatives.

The second practice of letting someone else manage the attribute is also known as "offloading" or "outsourcing" and commonly occurs when software organizations offload services or software to third-party providers. For example, a software organization making use of Amazon Web Services (AWS) to host applications or store data would fall under the classification of offloading to a third party. Such offloading is ubiquitous in the software community as third-party services offer convenience at competitive prices. An alternative to third-party services is conducting the service in-house, which could cost more and create significantly more hassle. Another consideration that encourages software organizations to offload is that any third-party services help alleviate some responsibility regarding privacy and security. For instance, a software organization that collects residents' movement data in a smart city would need to ensure that the data is securely stored in databases on the premises. However, if the organization is instead using a third-party database provider to manage data storage, the organization has much less responsibility. While the organization retains the responsibility to ensure that the databases in the cloud are finely tuned to not leak personal data, the organization is cleared from the day-to-day management of the privacy and security of the databases. The caveat with offloading is that a software organization most likely needs to pre-plan the location of the data storage. Many national and local governments have stringent restrictions on the physical location of data that require organizations to store data in specific jurisdictions. For example, universities in the province of British Columbia must abide by the Freedom of Information and Protection of Privacy Act (FIPPA), which requires that personal and personally identifiable data must be physically stored within Canada.

The third practice of writing your own tool to check the attribute is similar to the second practice. The main difference is that the organization develops its own tool instead of relying on a third-party service. Nonetheless, considering the cost of developing one's own tool, writing your own tool is often seen as a last resort for small, resource-constrained organizations. While it is much more economically feasible for an organization to sign up for a third-party service, the organization may be forced to customize. For example, an organization may develop its own monitoring system to ensure that data is collected as expected.

Finally, the last practice involves writing down an attribute in the software. As we will later discuss in this chapter, reaching an adequate level of shared understanding of privacy is difficult and so documenting and writing down necessary details as frequently as possible is beneficial to managing a privacy attribute. In the study by Werner et al. (2021), it was observed that developers often opted to record knowledge about a software attribute through codification or related artifacts. This approach is viewed positively, as developers perceive that they themselves and other developers can easily find the knowledge in the code base of the software.

3.3   Challenges with Managing Privacy Compliance

While the aforementioned practices can assist in managing privacy, several note-worthy challenges were found in the study regarding managing privacy. In particular, automation and shared understanding of software attributes are viewed as significant challenges.

3.3.1   Automation

Automation is a challenge, as not all privacy attributes are suitable for automated tests. Some attributes may be naturally difficult to test, leading to hindrances on the part of the developer to implement an automated framework to verify the attributes. For example, one area of concern regarding data collection is that a person's personal data should be accurate. However, verifying the accuracy of the data collected on the part of a data-gathering organization may be onerous, with some form of manual intervention. While it may be in a software organization's best interests to develop a tool to conduct automated testing of the important privacy attributes, the ease of developing clear testable metrics of the privacy attributes may be arduous. If the organization's developers also lack knowledge of privacy regulations, defining metrics of the privacy attributes may be further limited.

3.3.2   Shared Understanding of Privacy

One associated problem with any requirement, especially privacy, is that there is not an equal level of understanding amongst a group of people. That group of people may include developers, project managers, managers, or any other stakeholders. If we think about the term privacy on its own, it would be difficult to form the same definition amongst a group of people, as everyone has their own definition. Unfor-tunately, most software requirements focus on the functional aspects; for example, the user clicks X and Y is shown. Furthermore, writing privacy requirements is a difficult task, and the requirements may be hard to test. So, what ends up happening is that a data collecting software organization claims they are a privacy-compliant solution, but no one can point somewhere in the code to say, "there we have privacy," and no one can really test it, since the definition may be ambiguous.

One problem a data collecting software organization may face when dealing with privacy is how to interpret any existing privacy legislation, as this usually requires a lawyer to understand the language in the legislation. Unfortunately, not many software developers are lawyers—and not many lawyers are software developers. The language in which legislation is written is likely to further contribute to a lack of shared understanding.

A privacy requirement may be dictated by some legislation, a project manager might write their own interpretation of that requirement in some development task management tool, a developer might read that requirement and develop software that conforms to their own interpretation, and finally, a tester might read the requirement and look at the product to assess that the privacy requirement was completed. However, not every privacy requirement will suffer, as some privacy requirements might be easier to interpret, implement, and test; for example, a database must be encrypted using AES-256 encryption.

Continuous software engineering (CSE) focuses on a succession of rapid cycles whereby software is released frequently, often as multiple short releases per hour or even in minutes. CSE induces and encourages an environment that requires software organizations to be able to handle a fast-paced environment. Research in practice has shown that CSE typically favors the release of features that users can actually use (perhaps new features or correcting buggy previously released features). Aspects of software, such as privacy, that do not necessarily impact or affect a feature visible or accessible to a user ultimately fall to the wayside. Research has indicated a correlation between CSE and a decreased level of shared understanding amongst requirements that do not exhibit direct functionality to users, such as privacy (Werner et al. 2020).

A side effect of CSE (and the associated environment experiencing a fast pace of change) is a lowered level of domain knowledge and inadequate communication. Domain knowledge is the business-specific context required to compete in a particular domain. Lack of domain knowledge can cause a lack of shared understanding of software attributes if a data collecting software organization is entering a new, unfamiliar market where even a basic understanding would be beneficial. Reaching consensus on the priority of an obscure requirement, such as privacy, may be difficult due to a discrepancy in perceived importance between different units within the organization. Additionally, the importance of a privacy requirement might be lowered until privacy is demanded by a particular customer.

CSE may also limit the ability of employees to communicate. Often developers may be isolated from one another, even if they are working on the same solution. The lack of communication may be a systemic problem related to the lack of domain knowledge, or simply an oversight on the part of a developer or a software organization. Alternatively, a developer may make false assumptions about privacy and just assume that privacy has already been handled elsewhere and is not within their current scope. Finally, privacy could be such an all-encompassing requirement that everyone assumes somebody else would handle such an important requirement, despite a lack of any documentation or notice. Ultimately, a communication breakdown about privacy can be disastrous, especially if privacy is supposed to be a key component of such a project.

3.4   Solutions

We discussed at length the difficulties and challenges with managing privacy in software organizations that are involved in collecting or analyzing data for smart city projects but have not yet described possible solutions.

3.4.1   Developing a Shared Understanding

Before embarking on actually achieving privacy compliance, it is wise for a smart city developer to invest in building a shared understanding of privacy. The shared understanding should encompass a variety of stakeholders invested in building the smart city. In particular (and at the very least), project management, development, and legal teams should build an equal, shared understanding with respect to privacy.

The first stage would involve a number of lawyers: lawyers that are familiar with the local laws where the smart city will be located, lawyers who are experts in privacy compliance, lawyers with experience in software, and additional lawyers lacking domain knowledge to help uncover tacit knowledge (Niknafs and Berry 2013). These lawyers should start building a shared understanding of the local laws and privacy compliance amongst themselves, likely bringing in project management and development teams as the level of shared understanding is substantial. However, we must also recognize the difficulty in discerning some new privacy laws, even for seasoned lawyers. Some privacy laws, such as the General Data Protection Regulation (GDPR) enacted in the European Union, were purposefully written in a broad and ambiguous manner to account for potential future technological advances and to provide legal guidance for a multitude of industries. Notwithstanding the reasoning for the ambiguity existing in the GDPR, some software organizations adopt a rather pragmatic wait-and-see approach to new privacy regulations as they want to see the degree of penalties that privacy regulators inflict on violators before deciding the level of compliance preparedness they should adopt. Further complicating the ease of uncovering knowledge and awareness about privacy regulations is that developers are ultimately the employees who implement privacy attributes in software. Even if lawyers have an abundance of privacy knowledge to share with developers, the transfer of knowledge is not trivial. Lawyers typically have little technical training, and developers rarely have a background in law, which can inhibit communication between the two parties.

Next, there should be a large effort to purposefully disseminate privacy compliance information, using both formal and informal techniques. Unsurprisingly, these techniques require adequate communication and documentation to succeed. Achieving a high level of communication and documentation might seem trivial to accomplish but is often harder than anticipated, thus requiring special focus to ensure that the communication and documentation are effective in disseminating information.

Once development teams have built and are able to maintain a shared under-standing then a set of shared development standards should be designed and imple-mented to capture how privacy compliance will be documented, implemented, and met. The task of developing and sharing these standards requires a shared understanding to be built and maintained before development.

At this point, and only at this point, should actual development begin–incorpo-rating the standards to achieve privacy compliance. The reason that development cannot begin prior to developing a shared understanding of how to achieve privacy compliance is that privacy attributes are not able to be shoehorned in after the fact, especially with software. Software that meets high levels of privacy compliance must be designed with privacy compliance in mind from the get-go (Cavoukian 2009).

3.4.2 Achieving Privacy Compliance

At this point, a software organization can move towards realizing privacy compli-ance in the software. There are two critical components to any software organiza-tion building and maintaining a shared understanding of privacy compliance: docu-mentation and communication. While documentation and communication are two innocuous and recurrent terms repeated ad nauseam by any software organization aiming for success, achieving these tenets is not necessarily trivial. Documentation is often the crucial first step, but documentation is notoriously costly and expensive, especially for small organizations that may not have massive resources. Instead, there is a minimum level of privacy documentation that organizations may find more suit-able for their situation. How much privacy documentation is needed depends on the organization and the situation, which makes discerning the level of documentation required such a challenging task. The likely prudent approach that an organization can take is identifying and recording the specific criteria of a privacy attribute as well as the test case for verifying the completion of the attribute. To maximize the useful-ness of documentation, a software organization should aim to document the attributes deemed most valuable to the organization or otherwise most mission-critical to the organization's business.

Another aspect that closely relates to documentation is communication. Once documentation is created, it is essential to share the documentation with all relevant stakeholders. At this point, communication is vital for disseminating documentation and relevant information to stakeholders. There are numerous mediums to facilitate communication including video conferencing, face-to-face meetings, texting, phone calls, or even emails. Regardless of the medium of communication, one key compo-nent is support from management in guiding employees to disseminate knowledge. Additionally, management and other stakeholders should help prioritize the impor-tant privacy attributes that highly impact the organization. If communication only flows in a unilateral direction (i.e., top to bottom) where experienced employees offer important information to junior employees, but the reverse flow of information does not occur, the organization risks developing tacit knowledge that only a select few individuals become aware of and increasing the organization's "bus" factor, a measurement for how many team members need to suddenly disappear for a project to fail or suffer significant setbacks due to a lack of knowledge.

Once sufficient privacy documentation and communication is achieved in a software organization, the next step involves developing tool(s) to verify that the privacy attributes the organization documented and prioritized are realized. Closely related to the aforementioned third practice to help manage privacy, writing your own tool or using an existing tool, if such tool exists, is meant to help an organization check to see if privacy attributes are achieved on a continual basis. The logic for continual verification is simple. It is of little use to a software organization if a privacy attribute (e.g., personal data must be deleted after 30 days) deemed significant is only achieved for a brief period of time. A prioritized privacy attribute most likely fits the long-term interests of an organization, so it is in the software organization's best interests to effectively treat the privacy attribute long term. Therefore, a privacy compliance check that an organization conducts on a semi-annual or annual basis is not effective for achieving privacy compliance, as the organization has little insight into the state of compliance during the interval between compliance checks. Instead, the auspicious approach that an organization should adhere to is one where it continually checks to see that its software satisfies the privacy attributes clearly documented and communicated to all relevant stakeholders.

The type of tool to check for privacy compliance varies by the organization, as each organization may have a different list of prioritized privacy attributes and associated software. For example, an organization may develop a tool to automatically verify that the cloud infrastructure it deploys on third-party services complies with privacy attributes. However, developing a tool is only one step of continuous privacy compliance. The other critical element that an organization must not omit is deploying the tool to its production system so that the tool is automatically executed on a continual basis. To quote Martin Fowler, a pioneer in the continuous integration movement, "imperfect tests, run frequently, are much better than perfect tests that are never written at all" (Fowler 2006). If an organization develops a tool to check for privacy, but rarely executes the tool, then the tool contributes little to the organization's compliance. While the frequency of test execution is up to each organization to determine the best interval for its situation, weekly test executions seem reasonable in the general case.

3.5 Conclusion

Treatment of privacy is a vital issue for smart cities. It is necessary to have a clear plan for managing privacy attributes, especially if proponents of a smart city project want to assuage critics who worry about risks to privacy. More importantly, each software organization that plays a role in the smart city project, whether it assists in data collection or analysis, must adequately manage privacy. After all, the amount of data generated and analyzed in smart cities is unprecedented, thus a heightened focus must be placed on protecting personal privacy.

In this chapter, we discuss a few challenges that a software organization working on a smart city project may encounter when trying to manage privacy, but we also describe several practices that an organization can adopt to effectively manage privacy. Ultimately, such an organization must make privacy a high-priority initiative, as—without clear motivation and willpower—attention to privacy may not reach a sufficient level.

References

Cavoukian A (2009) Privacy by design: the 7 foundational principles. Information and Privacy Commissioner of Ontario, Canada

Earth.org (2021) Smart cities: Top 7 smart cities in the world and how they do it. https://earth.org/top-7-smart-cities-in-the-world/

Fowler M (2006) Continuous integration. https://martinfowler.com/articles/continuousIntegration.html. Accessed 4 Oct 2021

Niknafs A, Berry DM (2013) An industrial case study of the impact of domain ignorance on the effectiveness of requirements idea generation during requirements elicitation. In: 2013 21st IEEE international requirements engineering conference (RE), pp 279–283

Tuerk M (2019) How data will fuel smart cities. https://www.forbes.com/sites/miriamtuerk/2019/11/25/how-data-will-fuel-smart-cities/. Accessed 4 Oct 2021

Werner C et al (2020) The lack of shared understanding of non-functional requirements in continuous software engineering: accidental or essential? In: 2020 IEEE 28th international requirements engineering conference (RE), pp 90–101

Werner C et al (2021) Continuously managing NFRs: opportunities and challenges in practice. IEEE Trans Softw Eng

Woetzel J et al (2021) Smart city technology for a more liveable future | McKinsey. https://www.mckinsey.com/business-functions/operations/our-insights/smart-cities-digital-solutions-for-a-more-livable-future. Accessed 29 Sept 2021

Chapter 4
Smart City and Privacy Concerns During COVID-19: Lessons from Singapore, Malaysia, and Indonesia

Melinda Martinus

Abstract Although smart technologies for managing urban problems have gained traction in Southeast Asia, citizens, experts, and policymakers continue to express concerns over data protection and security. Smart technologies, such as big data, artificial intelligence, and the Internet of Things (IoT), are perceived as enablers for cities to control air pollution, reduce traffic, streamline public services, and make energy use more efficient. Yet experts underline that smart technologies' personal and behavioral data have not been adequately protected, thus bringing significant risk to individual privacy. However, the COVID-19 pandemic has further intensified the dialogue to address privacy concerns in the digital sphere. Drawing from the experience of COVID-19 tracing applications in Singapore, Malaysia, and Indonesia, this chapter finds that despite concerns about technical issues and accessibility, the practice of surveillance and the effectiveness of such technology adoption to fight COVID-19 remain in debate. The dialogue on data protection in the digital sphere has been more complex as there are contesting interests between the need to ensure public safety and the need to protect individual privacy.

4.1 Introduction

In recent years, the concept of the smart city has been gaining traction across cities around the globe. With many projections indicating that population growth in urban areas will only increase and cause further environmental-related challenges, many planners have proposed smart technology as a solution. Cities increasingly develop or adopt technology-led interventions such as big data, artificial intelligence, and the IoT to control urban problems, such as reducing air pollution and traffic, streamlining public services, and making energy use more efficient.

As a consequence of those interventions, urban citizens increasingly participate in those various digital platforms that further enable them to share their personal data

M. Martinus (✉)
ISEAS—Yusof Ishak Institute, 30 Heng Mui Keng Terrace, Singapore 119614, Singapore
e-mail: melinda_martinus@iseas.edu.sg

© The Author(s) 2022   33
T. Phan and D. Damian (eds.), *Smart Cities in Asia*, SpringerBriefs in Geography,
https://doi.org/10.1007/978-981-19-1701-1_4

and behavior to technology providers. This intensive use of technology has exposed them to data breaches, cyberattacks, and possibly the threat of public surveillance.

This paper seeks to understand the risk of smart city adoption intruding on individual privacy. Using various cases of data breaches, cyberattacks, and the threat of public surveillance in Southeast Asia, this chapter highlights the nexus of development policy, politics, and dynamic risks coming from smart city adoption. This chapter further analyzes the issue of digital privacy concerns during the COVID-19 pandemic by looking specifically at the adoption of digital tracing applications' challenges and opportunities in Singapore, Indonesia, and Malaysia.

4.2   Smart Cities Development Context in Southeast Asia

Southeast Asia will undoubtedly soon be the fastest growing market for smart cities. Today almost 50% of the region's population lives in cities. It is estimated that the region will achieve 56% urbanization by 2030 (United Nations 2018).

The region is home to youthful, digitally savvy, and upwardly mobile populations (Sheng 2019). It has seen a dramatic increase in internet usage in the past years. Currently, 60% of the population has access to the internet, and this rate is higher in countries such as Brunei (95%), Singapore (89%), Malaysia (84%), Vietnam (59%), and Thailand (67%) (Ingram 2020). Digital sectors, mainly e-commerce, transport and food, online travel, digital media, and financial services, are predicted to unleash the region's maximum growth. Google, Singapore wealth fund Temasek, and consultancy firm Bain & Co (2020) highlight that six countries of the region, Singapore, Indonesia, Malaysia, the Philippines, Thailand, and Vietnam, are on track to unlock a $300 billion internet economy by 2025.

In light of urbanization and economic opportunities from the digital sector, the region has been increasingly pursuing smart city aspirations as a national development premise. Singapore, the pioneer of the smart city movement in the region, spearheaded the Smart Nation initiative in 2014, a program to harness digital technologies to empower the economy and improve public services that respond to Singapore's citizens' different and changing needs (Smart Nation Singapore nd).

Other countries in the region, particularly Indonesia and Malaysia, have also mobilized smart city strategies as a national plan. In 2017, Indonesia's Ministry of Communication and Information Technology Indonesia launched the 100 Smart Cities Movement to address urbanization issues and improve the quality of life of urban citizens. The program aims to work on six key areas: governance, people, economy, mobility, living, and environment. Similarly, Malaysia's government recently spearheaded the Malaysia Smart City Framework (MSCF) to present a national document to guide Malaysia's innovative city development across states and regions. The MSCF is strategically aligned with other domestic plans such as an urbanization policy, a physical plan, green technology, low-carbon cities, and Malaysia's global commitment to the New Urban Agenda (the UN-Habitat) and the Sustainable Development Goals (SDG) (Lim et al. 2020).

The Philippines introduced New Manila Bay, a 407-ha city and a new integrated central business district (CBD) enhanced by artificial intelligence. New Manila Bay is the biggest Belt and Road project between the Philippines and China to date and is estimated to be completed in 2030 (Seow 2017). Another new development, New Clark City, is the country's first new town development that integrates smart, green, and resilient solutions to address climate change and natural disasters.

Thailand's government plans to adopt a smart city approach to enhance investment in cities along the Eastern Economic Corridor (EEC), a special economic zone with a solid manufacturing base (Dunseith 2018). As the government of Thailand expects to generate US$43 billion for the realization of the EEC, the government has been enhancing four investment areas: improved infrastructure, business and industrial clustering, tourism, and new town development through smart urban planning.

The push for the adoption of smart cities for urban development has also become a regional movement in Southeast Asia. Initiated by Singapore during its Association of Southeast Asian Nations (ASEAN) chairmanship in 2018, the ASEAN Smart City Network (ASCN) was launched as a network of 26 pilot cities from all 10 ASEAN member states to work towards the common goal of smart and sustainable urban development. The network facilitates knowledge exchange and capacity building among the pilot cities and pairs them up with donors, solution providers, and the private sector. The network works on six service domains: civic and social, health and wellbeing, safety and security, quality environment, built infrastructure, and industry and innovation (Centre for Liveable Cities 2018). Some of the projects proposed by the pilot cities are e-health and telemedicine services for rural areas in Makassar, Indonesia; an integrated e-payment system in Singapore; converged command and control services for enhancing public safety in Davao, Philippines; and smart manufacturing and logistics in Chonburi, Thailand.

4.3   Smart City and Privacy Concerns

As smart cities have undoubtedly gained traction in the region, one concern emerging from their implementation is privacy, especially how service providers maintain integrity by protecting users' data. As the smart city facilitates interconnectivity between users and providers, data will be transferred and utilized through various processes, which often involves multiple parties communicating and gaining access to data (Braun et al. 2018). This complex interaction will certainly endanger users' privacy. The way information is managed and stored by authorities could also bring security threats, as it simultaneously links data with new sensors and systems of the latest smart technologies (van Zoonen 2016). Furthermore, data is stored and distributed across multiple devices, locations, and service providers, and this could, in turn, add complexities in managing an increased amount of personal data generated from smart applications (Rosadi et al. 2017). In Southeast Asia, data breaching concerns involving public services and smart technologies have appeared in several instances.

One landmark case is the data breach of the MyKad project in Malaysia. In 2001, the government of Malaysia launched a multipurpose national digital identity card as a validation tool and proof of citizenship other than the birth certificate. MyKad was projected to replace the old identity card—*Kad Pengenalan Bermutu Tinggi*—as a valid identity card for Malaysian citizens and permanent residents over 12 years old. As digitalization became a flagship national project and was predicted to help Malaysia achieve developed nation status, the MyKad project had become a critical national program (Thomas 2004).

When the government introduced the project, the people of Malaysia generally gave substantial support and showed enthusiasm for the program, as MyKad was intended to simplify four types of personal identity: the national identity card, driving license, passport application, and health information. The government of Malaysia set aside a RM 276 million budget (US$67 million) and selected the National Registration Department (NRD) as the lead government agency and several companies to expedite the implementation (Thomas 2004).

MyKad was developed as a converged identity card, where authorized Government Service Centres (GSCs) such as the NRD, the Road Transport Department, the Immigration Department, and the Royal Transport Department can read, write, print, and utilize specific information on the MyKad. The card is equipped with an intelligent chip and up-to-date biometric technology, such as a colored digital photograph and a digital scan of the cardholder's thumbprint in the chip. GSCs's mandate then includes front-to-end data management, which handles the application process, data storage, and communication with the database centers, which the NRD hosts.

As a result of this digital feature, the personal information in MyKad can be accessed by certain government agencies or selected third parties who have the appropriate access rights. Also, any grant of access rights to the various authorities and third parties have thus far been done administratively and without transparency or public disclosure (Thomas 2004). Another hurdle is that the *National Registration Act* 1959 and *National Registration Regulation* 1990 do not indicate explicitly what types of information or database access are restricted (Thomas 2004).

The issue of privacy in the MyKad case continued to attract public attention when the Malaysian government indicated that in the future, the card could facilitate online transactions such as the digital wallet, ATM access, and transit applications. Consequently, MyKad would not serve solely as a digital identity card but as a multipurpose card with considerable capacity for expansion to other domains (Thomas 2004). As such, data and privacy protection must be seriously addressed and standardized by regulations.

Another privacy issue in the smart city domain involves concerns over cyberattacks. Vendors of service providers usually deploy software and complex infrastructure for smart cities without sufficient cybersecurity standards; thus, when interacting with such equipment, users may be exposed to several hacks and malicious software variants (AlDairi and Tawalbeh 2017). The most common type of cybersecurity threats in smart cities are denial of service attacks, unauthorized network access, theft of personal information, online financial fraud, website defacement, application-layer attacks such as cross-site scripting, and penetration attacks (Bélanger and Carter 2008).

Cases of cyberattack and data breach appeared in the recent attack involving Indonesia's super app, Tokopedia. Tokopedia has been considered a champion of "shared economy" in the smart city era—along with the giant ride-hailing companies of Gojek and Grab—because its business model provides an e-commerce platform for small and medium enterprises (SMEs). With such a platform, individuals can now sell their goods and services by utilizing the internet and electronic devices. Tokopedia collaborates with various government services such as the State Electricity Company (PLN), the Municipal Waterworks (PDAM), and the National Gas Company to facilitate municipal services and payment subscriptions. Tokopedia's platform indeed revolutionizes municipal services as the super app helps increase accessibility and efficiency of government services in dealing with customers.

Currently, Tokopedia has more than 10 million sellers and 100 million active transactions every month. According to Tokopedia's website, 90% of the sellers enjoy the digital transactions provided by the super app. In order to participate in Tokopedia, customers must register using their mobile phone number or email address. Customers are invited to provide their valid address, date of birth, bank account, credit or debit card, or any information about their preferred payment. Customers also need to provide an identity card for verification. Consequently, they are releasing their essential personal data and financial information to enjoy services provided by Tokopedia.

In May 2020, Tokopedia confirmed that it experienced a single cyberattack that attempted to steal 15 million users' data from its super app (Eloksari 2020). The case had become the first and largest data leak involving the e-commerce sector in the country. In a statement to the Jakarta Post, a cybersecurity research group asserted that this cyberattack happened because Tokopedia has too many employees with access to the company's internal system (Eloksari 2020). Besides, many tech-companies that provide super apps like Tokopedia often rely heavily on third-party companies that integrate with their systems, which increases the vulnerability to hacking.

In response to customers' concerns, Tokopedia claimed that the cyberattack only attempted to steal data from its servers but assured customers that their passwords were still protected and no payment information had been leaked (Fachriansyah 2020). Customers were encouraged to change their password to ensure safety. However, some experts argued that although hackers did not steal password and payment information, some primary data that were hacked, such as phone numbers and email addresses, are also sensitive to cybercrime (Fachriansyah 2020). That information can further facilitate spam and phishing. Customers have the rights to data protection, and service providers must ensure that they are accountable.

In a similar sense, privacy and smart city issues also include concerns over freedom of personal space and threats of surveillance as the result of technology adoption. Unlike data breach threats and cyberattacks that threaten personal data, the threats of surveillance interface with people in public spaces in a direct way. People's privacy is exposed to an increasing degree as many cities have increasingly deployed hardware such as public cameras, traffic control, and facial-recognition tools to increase the city's responsiveness to crimes, vandalism, accidents, and many types of disruptions in public spaces.

Such technology deployment would not only perpetuate surveillance by authority but dramatically change the normative assumptions about society's conception of human behavior in public spaces (Graham 2002). It would be more common to embed opaque codes in computer systems in calculating exposure of risk of an individual. Further, surveillance technology would normalize certain behavior because governments, through their matrix calculation, now can draw a line between "acceptable" and "unacceptable" behavior (Graham 2002).

In the Philippines, the issue over privacy and public surveillance emerged when the Philippines' government introduced the Safe Philippines Project or the Safe PH Project—a flagship program led by the Department of the Interior and Local Government (DILG). The program aims to provide crime prevention measures by utilizing high-definition and advanced closed-circuit television (CCTV) to help authorities monitor the occurrence of crimes, identify perpetrators, and improve emergency response time (Caliwan 2019).

The project received unwavering support as crime has been touted as a critical problem in many cities in the Philippines. A government official claimed that the country could attain peace and order in the community and invite more investors to do businesses by improving safety and security in the public space. In one sense, this program will indeed sustain economic growth and jobs in the Philippines (Caliwan 2019).

However, the project was received with much resistance when President Duterte and President Xi Jinping of China called for a collaboration between Chinese technology providers (potentially Huawei) and local authorities in the Philippines (Mandhana 2019). The agreement confirmed a plan to provide 12,000 closed-circuit televisions and facial-recognition technology in Manila and Davao (Mandhana 2019). It remained unclear which Chinese technology provider would provide such hardware. However congressional opponents in the Philippines expressed concerns over the involvement of a third-party service provider from China, notably Huawei.

Huawei is best known to provide cutting-edge telecommunication technologies, especially mobile phones, 5G network equipment, and the IoT across the region. Their technology and low cost unarguably help many developing countries in achieving smart city aspirations. Nonetheless, over the years, Huawei's reputation got tarnished as many lawmakers and security-threat experts from Western countries increasingly conveyed concerns over its technology that could be exploited by the Chinese government, presenting a potentially grave national security risk (Lecher and Brandom 2019). Moreover, the Philippines and China's relationship is often troubled when it comes to strategic and political affairs. The two countries have long been in dispute over maritime boundaries in the South China Sea.

When asked about the concerns about Chinese technology, a senator from the Philippines asserted that if the Philippines' government wants to select vendors for critical infrastructure like closed-circuit television and facial-recognition technologies, it must not select Chinese vendors (Mandhana 2019). The case of concerns over third-party intrusions in the Philippines' surveillance system has underlined the importance of having standardized guidelines for selecting service vendors. As surveillance systems require high integrity in analyzing data gathered from hardware and potentially expose individuals' identity and behaviors in the public domain, the third-party vendors who provide the service must comply with regulations, particularly compliance with ethical procedures.

There is no doubt that the adoption of smart technology will bring with it risks to privacy. The cases of digital privacy intrusion in the form of data breaches, cyberattacks, and digital surveillance across Southeast Asia have become a public concern.

While policies to create a safety ecosystem are still being developed, the COVID-19 pandemic has completely altered the debate over this issue. To help to limit the spread of the coronavirus, policymakers suggest or even mandate the use of technology, for instance contact tracing applications. Users' participation in such technology use is encouraged despite there still being limited frameworks to shield privacy.

4.4   Public Safety and Privacy During COVID-19

The increasing adoption of various smart city technologies has undoubtedly brought personal data infringement concerns into the digital sphere. However, it was not until the COVID-19 pandemic loomed in the region that policymakers have given more attention to public safety and privacy, facilitated more dialogue, and intensified various efforts to improve laws and regulations in managing such challenges.

COVID-19 was declared a global pandemic by the World Health Organization (WHO) on 11 March 2020. As a measure to curb the spread of the virus, policymakers have utilized numerous digital technology measures, namely data monitoring systems, contact tracing, and health screening. Contract tracing, which has been widely deployed across the region, works to help health officials identify and track individuals who might have come into contact with an infected person. To do so, users must install the application on their mobile phones or wearables. The tracing application utilizes global positioning systems or Bluetooth devices on users' mobile phones, thus facilitating signal exchanges between phones.

The adoption of such measures requires voluntary participation from users. From the perspective of public safety, adopting such a technology helps health officials to act promptly. Users who are in close contact with people infected with COVID-19 will receive notification via the app, messages, and emails that they need to monitor their health condition. Other information such as quarantine guidelines, supportive services, testing, and clinical care services are also provided to assist users further to minimize the risk of transmission. Such measures are considered necessary as the COVID-19 vaccine has not yet been widely distributed at the time of writing this chapter.

However, the adoption of contact tracing is not without risks. To participate in the application, users must reveal their identity, such as an address, phone number, and household information, and also exchange their travel patterns, thus increasing personal data breach exposure. This issue has become a concern in the case of TraceTogether (Singapore), MySejahtera (Malaysia), and Peduli Lindungi (Indonesia).

4.4.1 Singapore: TraceTogether

On 20 March 2020, Singapore's government released the TraceTogether application as a measure to enhance Singapore's contact tracing efforts. The app helps to more efficiently identify people who are in proximity to an infected person using the proximity data collected. Using Bluetooth technology, TraceTogether works by approximating the distance between users by measuring the strength of the signals received from other Bluetooth devices (tracetogether.gov.sg nd). This approximation further allows the application to calculate the length of communication between devices.

Although digital access is ubiquitous in Singapore, approximately 20% of its population is still underserved (Eigen and Gasser 2020). Hence, when the app was launched, it received criticism for not being accessible to those who do not possess a smartphone, especially the poor, the elderly, and children. These groups are also the ones who are the most susceptible to the virus. To make this application more accessible, the government introduced the TraceTogether token on 28 June and distributed it to 10,000 seniors (Eigen and Gasser 2020).

As of June 2020, three months after the app was introduced, the program received low participation from citizens. Less than a quarter of Singapore's population or only 1,800,000 people downloaded the application (Baharudin and Yip 2020). Meanwhile, to work properly, the application needs at least 75% of the population to use the app to increase density and allow more information exchange between mobile phones. When asked about this issue, Singapore's minister in charge of the Smart Nation Initiative pointed out that low participation was due to technical difficulties on iPhone or Apple devices (Baharudin 2020).

There was also a changing policy on ensuring compliance. When the application was introduced, participation was entirely voluntary. As an effort to increase participation among Singapore's residents, the government mandated the TraceTogether app or token be used at popular venues such as cinemas, workplaces, schools, and shopping malls. The government had also increased the number of tokens distributed to residents to encourage more participation (Wong 2020a).

In a statement, Singapore's education minister asserted that 70% adoption could help Singapore reach its next reopening level (Wong 2020a). However, this percentage of adoption can be achieved only through legal compulsion. The government will only get data from people who consent; however, if users do not consent, they could be prosecuted under Singapore's Infectious Disease Act (Ng 2020). The act mandates the public authorities in charge with the responsibility for regulation of diseases and disease control. Any action that could hinder or obstruct the public authority to do so could be an offense according to the Infectious Disease Act (Global-is-asian 2020).

The issue of privacy first appeared when nearly 40,000 people signed a petition highlighting the poor interoperability of the existing TraceTogether smartphone app across various brands of smartphones (Low, nd). Most importantly, the petition underlined concerns over the wearable device's (token) 24/7 surveillance. However, government officials responded to this false suspicion. TraceTogether would not allow contact tracers to locate a person's location based on their proximity to other users' devices because the token does not have GPS or internet connectivity (Global-is-asian 2020).

The government of Singapore stated that TraceTogether is different from a tracking device or an electronic tag. The government improved TraceTogether's privacy safeguards, such as storing data limited to mobile phone number, identification details, and user ID only. A user's personal information is stored on a secure server and never shown to the public. Users are allowed to request to delete data from the server. The government also ensured that third-party services would not access users' data. The tracking data stored in the personal devices will be stored no longer than 25 days according to the TraceTogether privacy safeguards. The evolution of Trace-Together's privacy safeguards shows that the Singaporean government acknowledged the strength of public attitudes and the importance of privacy and data protection concerns and sought to anticipate debates by building in some level of privacy protection (Goggin 2020).

The privacy safeguard design of TraceTogether was "fairly elegant" and "preserves a fair degree of privacy" (Goggin 2020). In several interviews, Singaporean government officials ensured that when the pandemic is over, people will get instructions to destroy their data to ensure safety. It is not surprising that TraceTogether received much praise for its innovation. Gartner, a market research firm, made TraceTogether the Asia–Pacific winner for its 2020 Government Eye on Innovation award based on a poll of government organizations worldwide (Wong 2020b). TraceTogether is not a silver bullet to curb the spread of the coronavirus, yet its ability to widely reach and consistently track possible close contacts should augment human contact-tracers' efforts (Asher 2020).

All the praise received by TraceTogether is not without challenges. Recently, TraceTogether came under fire after authorities disclosed that police used the data for a murder investigation—after the government released a statement that the application will only be used for COVID-19 containment (Tarabay 2021). After a public outcry, Singapore's parliament passed a bill restricting the use of personal contact tracing data to serious criminal investigations only (Chee 2021). Singapore's minister in charge of the Smart Nation Initiative stated that limiting the use of contact tracing data within the proposed law is "a result of a delicate balance between the right to public health, the right to public security, and respecting the sensitivity of personal data during this extraordinary time" (Chee 2021).

4.4.2 Malaysia: MySejahtera

In order to eliminate the spread of COVID-19, the Malaysian government launched MySejahtera, a centralized portal that allows residents to monitor their health and share it with the Ministry of Health. It consists of several features that include self-assessment, a COVID-19 hotspot map, statistics of COVID-19 cases, information on health facilities, and a QR code scan for checking in at the premises. Recently, the government also announced that the application can be used for vaccine registration (Yeoh 2021).

Although MySejahtera is developed by federal government agencies and is mandatory for all businesses in Malaysia, several states also developed their own QR-based contact tracing. These applications include those developed by SELangkah (Selangor), SabahTrace (Sabah), CovidIDtrace (Sarawak), and PgCare (Penang) (Said 2020). The contact tracing application in Malaysia is rather non-homogeneous, and several states demonstrated strong governance in their localities (Said 2020).

MySejahtera faced various technical difficulties. First, as the cases of COVID-19 reached four-figure increases daily in early 2021, the health officials became overwhelmed in facilitating help for suspected cases. Many people claimed they had not received assistance, although they had already filed a report to health officials. Although the app was supported widely by the federal government, the government still needed thousands of physical contact traces. At least 30 tracers per 100,000 were still required to free up existing health professionals (Sukumaran 2021). These physical contact tracers could consist of professional personnel or volunteers.

Second, there was a concern about external parties' involvement when the application was launched. According to its website, MySejahtera was developed by strategic cooperation between the National Security Council (NSC), the Ministry of Health (MOH), the Malaysian Administrative Modernization and Management Planning Unit (MAPU), the Malaysian Communications and Multimedia Commission (MCMC), and the Ministry of Science, Technology and Innovation (MOSTI). However, there is no clear information on whether the app was developed internally by the government agencies or whether any external vendor was involved in the development. MySejahtera failed to provide more details regarding this concern (FocusM 2020).

Among the concerns raised, the issue of privacy seems to be the most prominent one. To register in MySejahtera, users need to provide a great deal of personal information, such as contact number, email address, full name, identity card, age, gender, ethnicity, and home address. To operate fully, the application requires access to smartphones' cameras, Bluetooth, flashlight, and full internet network access. Personal data privacy has always been a big issue in Malaysia, as the country experienced several data breach cases in the digital sphere. One of the most recent ones was the leak of 46 million mobile phone numbers from mobile operators and various professional associations, affecting the entire country (BBC 2017).

A research report from the Asia Pacific Training Centre for Information and Communication Technology for Development (APCICT/ESCAP) also highlights that MySejatera has not yet stated how personal data is processed and offers little explanation on how permissions are being used in the app (APCICT/ESCAP 2020).

Digital security experts also raised a concern about the power balance between government control and citizens' rights to personal privacy. Although the application must adhere to the Personal Data Protection Act (PDPA) 2010—the national act that regulates the procession of personal data to comply with certain obligations—the government is not subject to the law. Under PPDPA 2010, the government is not accountable for any data leaks, cyberattacks, or other breaches due to negligence (OneTrust Data Guidance 2020).

Experts also raised concerns about the efficacy of MySejahtera if it is balanced against concerns of privacy and personal choice. For instance, although the government periodically stated that the application had helped the government to identify COVID-19 cases, the government did not clarify whether the cases were from people who were mandated to download the app from the voluntary download.

4.4.3   Indonesia: PeduliLindungi

Like TraceTogether and MySejahtera, Indonesia launched PeduliLindungi in late March, 2020 to curb the spread of the coronavirus. The application, developed by the Ministry of Communications and Information and the Ministry of State-Owned Enterprises (SOEs), utilizes a Bluetooth connection to detect another user whose data has been uploaded to PerduliLindungi's servers. This detection could help enable the exchange of data. If a user is found near confirmed suspected cases, the application will prompt a notification.

There were some technical issues when the program was introduced. As of April 2020, the application was installed by a couple of million people, although Indonesia has more than 100 million smartphone users (Florene 2020). Meanwhile, to work properly, contact tracing apps need approximately three-quarters of the population to install the application. Experts indicate that this requirement is due to the application not providing much information (Florene 2020). The application only points out a risky zone without details about the risk and the number of cases in each area.

When the application was introduced, the privacy concern also quickly gained ground. A group of human rights organizations addressed an open letter to the Indonesian minister of communication and information technology, demanding more privacy safeguards. When the application was launched, no application privacy safeguard was stated under the App Store or Google Play. The experts also requested the government release the white paper and source code for the PeduliLindungi application, provide a clear privacy policy, issue data privacy regulations, provide information about a recent data breach, and take steps to protect the right to privacy (Jakarta Post 2020).

There is also a concern over the risk of malware in the use of the PeduliLindungi application. As the application requires users to keep activating their Bluetooth, there is a risk of a malware attack for those who do not regularly update their Bluetooth application (Wira 2020). In general, when users start their Bluetooth and pair their phone to another phone, they must receive a notification. However, there is no such feature for users who do not have the latest version of Bluetooth. Malware can steal confidential information stored in a phone, such as password and credit card details.

Constant surveillance by the government was also another concern, as the application constantly notifies users if they are in crowded areas or zones with many cases (APCICT/ESCAP 2020). There are no detailed explanations of the technicalities of data acquisition in the application, as it seemed to utilize both Bluetooth and geolocation at the same time. Unlike Singapore's TraceTogether application that uses a single Bluetooth tracing method without acquiring geolocation data, PeduliLindungi's application seems to be much riskier.

A report from the Citizen Lab, Munk School of Global Affairs, shows that Indonesia's PeduliLindungi might acquire too much unnecessary data, risking more personal privacy while having less effectivity in minimizing the spread of the virus (Lin et al. 2020). According to the report, the application collected a great deal of data, such as geolocation, permission to take photos and video, and permission to access users' storage to allow the application to read users' photos and files. These are unnecessary data as tracing applications need only to communicate with other devices when in proximity.

However, the biggest concern is the way geolocation data is collected and managed, according to the report. The government selected Telkom Indonesia's server to store the end-point data. Appointing a third-party provider to oversee data will only increase the risk of a data breach. Data such as users' geolocations, Wi-Fi Mac addresses, users' phone numbers, and users' full names are stored in the third-party server, although none of these is necessary for contact tracing (Lin et al. 2020). TraceTogether, instead, can maximize the use of Bluetooth to detect nearby devices, especially those who are COVID-19 positive and to identify crowded areas.

Although the Indonesian government specifically regulated the use of TraceTogether through two decrees, Indonesia, in general, is still lacking comprehensive privacy laws in the digital sphere. For instance, there is no specific law that regulates punitive measures for parties who initiate a data breach. The current regulation only contains administrative sanctions such as oral and written warnings, temporary suspensions, and mandated announcements on the mass media (Florene 2020).

The COVID-19 pandemic has indeed further intensified the dialogue to address privacy concerns in the digital sphere. How this issue continues to evolve and what kind of interventions will be developed are still too early to predict. But the pandemic raises the question of whether protecting privacy must be absolute or whether it can be flexible in a time of crisis. If it can be flexible, to what extent should governments or the appointed authorities gather and use public data for the public interest, for example, monitoring the spread of disease, protecting citizens' health, and keeping the social order? And most importantly, how can we balance the urgency of maintaining public safety with the needs of protecting individual privacy?

4.5 Conclusion

There are indeed contested interests between the need to ensure public safety from the pandemic and privacy infringement concerns. However, some governments across the region have realized that there are increasing public concerns about privacy protection in the digital sphere. Most importantly, the case of contact tracing adoption across the region has indicated that many governments are demonstrating some efforts in building trust, namely improving written privacy safeguards and more transparency on the way users' data is managed, accessed, and stored. There are few things to take note of.

First, lawmakers must be clear in defining to what extent the law on privacy protection prevails above other laws. In Singapore's case, for instance, the law on privacy protection was adjusted in order to comply with any legal obligations, such as criminal law and laws on infectious disease. This adjustment will help the regulators and the public be better informed when there is a need to compromise the risk of privacy for public safety.

Second, there must be clear punitive measures for every stakeholder involved in data breaches. Privacy protection law must better state punishments for those who breach the laws without exception. As a preventive measure, if possible, law must limit the stakeholders involved in data processing and storing.

Third, as smart city adoption is becoming more complex and will involve many stakeholders in the future, there is a need to build more complex data protection layering. Regulators could oblige service providers by designing multiple components of data processing, so that there is a better opportunity to break attempts to breach data.

References

AlDairi A, Tawalbeh L (2017) Cyber security attacks on smart cities and associated mobile technologies. Procedia Comput Sci 109:1086–1091. https://doi.org/10.1016/j.procs.2017.05.391

APCICT/ESCAP (2020) Resource materials on "data privacy laws in Asia and the Pacific." UNAPCICT. https://www.unapcict.org/resources/publications/resource-materials-data-privacy-laws-asia-and-pacific

Asher (2020) TraceTogether: Singapore turns to wearable contact-tracing Covid tech. BBC News

Baharudin H (2020) Wearable device for Covid-19 contact tracing to be rolled out soon, may be issued to everyone in Singapore, Politics News & Top Stories—The Straits Times. The Straits Times

Baharudin H, Yip WY (2020) Coronavirus: 25% of TraceTogether users update app to latest version. The Straits Times

BBC (2017) Malaysian data breach sees 46 million phone numbers leaked. https://www.bbc.com/news/technology-41816953. Accessed 5 Apr 2021

Bélanger F, Carter L (2008) Trust and risk in e-government adoption. J Strateg Inf Syst 17:165–176. https://doi.org/10.1016/j.jsis.2007.12.002

Braun T, Fung BCM, Iqbal F, Shah B (2018) Security and privacy challenges in smart cities. Sustain Cities Soc 39:499–507. https://doi.org/10.1016/j.scs.2018.02.039

Caliwan CL (2019) DILG launches "safe PH project" in Marikina. https://www.pna.gov.ph/articles/ 1086797. Accessed 5 Apr 2021

Centre for Liveable Cities (2018) ASEAN smart cities network. Singapore

Chee K (2021) Bill limiting police use of TraceTogether data to serious crimes passed. Politics News & Top Stories—The Straits Times. The Straits Times

Dunseith B (2018) Thailand's eastern economic corridor—what you need to know. ASEAN Business News. https://www.aseanbriefing.com/news/thailand-eastern-economic-corridor/. Accessed 5 Apr 2021

Eigen M, Gasser U (2020) Country spotlight: Singapore's TraceTogether program. https://cyber. harvard.edu/story/2020-07/country-spotlight-singapores-tracetogether-program. Accessed 5 Apr 2021

Eloksari EA (2020) Tokopedia data breach exposes vulnerability of personal data. The Jakarta Post. https://www.thejakartapost.com/news/2020/05/04/tokopedia-data-breach-exposes-vulnerability-of-personal-data.html. Accessed 5 Apr 2021

Fachriansyah R (2020) Data breach jeopardizes more than 15 million Tokopedia users, report finds. The Jakarta Post. https://www.thejakartapost.com/news/2020/05/03/data-breach-jeopar dizes-more-than-15-million-tokopedia-users-report-finds.html. Accessed 5 Apr 2021

Florene U (2020) Indonesians skeptical of the state's COVID-19 prevention apps. KrASIA

FocusM (2020) MySejahtera privacy, safety concerns remain unaddressed. Focus Malaysia. https://focusmalaysia.my/mainstream/mysejahtera-privacy-safety-concerns-remain-unaddr essed/. Accessed 5 Apr 2021

Global-is-asian (2020) Public health or privacy concern? The debate over contact-tracing apps. Global Is Asian. https://lkyspp.nus.edu.sg/gia/video/public-health-or-privacy-concern-the-deb ate-over-contact-tracing-apps. Accessed 5 Apr 2021

Goggin G (2020) COVID-19 apps in Singapore and Australia: reimagining healthy nations with digital technology. Media Int Aust 177:61–75. https://doi.org/10.1177/1329878X20949770

Google, Temasek, Bain & Company (2020) e-Conomy SEA 2020. https://www.bain.com/insights/ e-conomy-sea-2020/

Graham S (2002) CCTV: the stealthy emergence of a fifth utility? Plan Theory Pract 3:237–241. https://doi.org/10.1080/14649350220150116

Ingram G (2020) Development in Southeast Asia: opportunities for donor collaboration. The digital world. Center for Sustainable Development at Brookings

Jakarta Post (2020) Human rights groups urge privacy protection in COVID-19 contact tracing efforts. The Jakarta Post

Lecher C, Brandom R (2019) Is Huawei a security threat? Seven experts weigh in. The Verge. https://www.theverge.com/2019/3/17/18264283/huawei-security-threat-experts-china-spying-5g. Accessed 5 Apr 2021

Lim SB, Abdul Malek J, Hussain M, Tahir Z (2020) Malaysia smart city framework: a trusted framework for shaping smart Malaysian Citizenship? Handbook of Smart Cities. Springer. pp 1–24. https://link.springer.com/referenceworkentry/10.1007%2F978-3-030-15145-4_34-1

Lin P, Knockel J, Poetranto I et al (2020) Unmasked II: an analysis of Indonesia and the Philippines' government-launched COVID-19 Apps. Citizen Lab, Munk School of Global Affairs and Public Policy, University of Toronto. https://citizenlab.ca/2020/12/unmasked-ii-an-analysis-of-indone sia-and-the-philippines-government-launched-covid-19-apps/

Low W (nd) Sign the petition. Change.org. https://www.change.org/p/singapore-government-sin gapore-says-no-to-wearable-devices-for-covid-19-contact-tracing. Accessed 5 Apr 2021

Mandhana N (2019) Huawei's video surveillance business hits snag in Philippines. Wall Street Journal

Ng A (2020) Coronavirus pandemic changes how your privacy is protected. CNET

OneTrust Data Guidance (2020) Malaysia—data protection overview. DataGuidance. https://www. dataguidance.com/notes/malaysia-data-protection-overview. Accessed 5 Apr 2021

Rosadi SD, Suhardi, Kristyan SA (2017) Privacy challenges in the application of smart city in Indonesia. In: 2017 international conference on information technology systems and innovation (ICITSI), pp 405–409

Said (2020) From the ground up: Malaysia's digital space amidst a pandemic. LSE Southeast Asia Blog. https://blogs.lse.ac.uk/seac/2020/11/16/from-the-ground-up-malaysias-digital-space-amidst-a-pandemic/. Accessed 5 Apr 2021

Seow J (2017) Manila's new smart city run by artificial intelligence. https://www.indesignlive.sg/projects/manilas-new-smart-city-run-artificial-intelligence. Accessed 5 Apr 2021

Sheng A (2019) Why Asean holds the edge in a digital future: it's the youth factor. South China Morning Post

Smart Nation Singapore Transforming Singapore (nd) Default. https://www.smartnation.gov.sg/why-Smart-Nation/transforming-singapore. Accessed 5 Apr 2021

Sukumaran T (2021) Why Malaysia's contact-tracing efforts are falling dangerously short. South China Morning Post

Tarabay J (2021) Countries vowed to restrict use of COVID-19 data. For one government, the temptation was too great. Fortune

Thomas M (2004) Is Malaysia's MyKad the "one card to rule them all"? the urgent need to develop a proper legal framework for the protection of personal information in Malaysia. Social Science Research Network, Rochester, NY

tracetogether.gov.sg (nd) TraceTogether privacy safeguards. https://www.tracetogether.gov.sg. Accessed 5 Apr 2021

United Nations (2018) The World's Cities in 2018

van Zoonen L (2016) Privacy concerns in smart cities. Gov Inf Q 33:472–480. https://doi.org/10.1016/j.giq.2016.06.004

Wira NN (2020) What to know before using PeduliLindungi surveillance app, according to cybersecurity expert. The Jakarta Post

Wong L (2020a) TraceTogether programme wins international award for innovative use of tech. The Straits Times

Wong L (2020b) TraceTogether check-ins to be compulsory at public venues in S'pore by end-December. The Straits Times. https://www.straitstimes.com/singapore/checking-in-with-tracetogether-to-be-compulsory-at-public-venues-by-december. Accessed 5 Apr 2021

Yeoh A (2021) MySejahtera now shows vaccine registration progress. The Star: Malaysia News

Chapter 5
Does Hong Kong Need a Coherent Policy on Cross Border Data Flows to Really Be Smart?

Ronald Ker-Wei Yu and Bryan Mercurio

Abstract Data flows are becoming ever more important to smart cities. Owing to the plethora of interconnections, an action in one area can result in unintended consequences elsewhere–and while a holistic approach to managing data and data flows sounds desirable, it remains to be seen whether such an approach is achievable. This chapter will explore the conflicting legal and other issues smart cities face, including how to provide access to tools and data to enable creation of apps, content, or products and adapt products for local and global needs; how to encourage use and deployment of data-dependent systems such as artificial intelligence (AI); and how to allow companies to fulfil obligations to provide customer support, enable commercial transactions or the flow of digital currencies. Using Hong Kong as a case study, the chapter overviews Hong Kong's quest to be a smart city, measures its progress against an objective, then evaluates the potential downsides of Hong Kong's laissez-faire approach to regulation before advocating for the establishment of a coordinated framework and policy for managing cross-border data flows.

5.1 Introduction

As smart cities complete the build-up of information technology (IT) infrastructure and as more smart devices are connected, data flows will become more important—not just intra-city flows but also external flows. To remain relevant and competitive, a smart city must rely on external data not only for short-term commercial needs, such as international payment transactions, but also for support and updates for smart devices and vehicles, long-term innovation, content creation, product development,

R. K.-W. Yu (✉)
Faculty of Law, The Chinese University of Hong Kong, 41 Ha Shan Kai Wat Fanling NT, Shatin, Hong Kong
e-mail: Ronba.hk@gmail.com

B. Mercurio
Faculty of Law, The Chinese University of Hong Kong, Room 638, Lee Shau Kee Building, Shatin, New Territories, Hong Kong
e-mail: b.mercurio@cuhk.edu.hk

© The Author(s) 2022
T. Phan and D. Damian (eds.), *Smart Cities in Asia*, SpringerBriefs in Geography,
https://doi.org/10.1007/978-981-19-1701-1_5

and business viability. This requirement concurrently involves legal issues connected with privacy, trade, e-commerce, finance and cybersecurity, and intellectual property, which, in turn, is further complicated by the need to protect data, enforce laws, and access tools for the creation of new content or innovations.

Data today is so ubiquitous, and systems are so interconnected, parties' actions in one digital domain can derail initiatives in another area. For instance, Facebook's cryptocurrency Libra largely failed because of distrust of Facebook's social media activities, notably with regards to its lack of protection of users' privacy (Mendoza 2020). What is now clear is that actions in one area can result in unintended consequences elsewhere—and while a holistic approach to managing data and data flows sounds desirable, it remains to be seen whether such an approach is achievable.

This chapter will examine the conflicting legal and other issues smart cities face, including how to provide access to tools and data to enable creation of apps, content, or products and adapt products for local and global needs; how to encourage use and deployment of data-dependent systems such as artificial intelligence (AI); and how to allow companies to fulfil obligations to provide customer support, enable commercial transactions, or the flow of digital currencies. Finally, this chapter explores how a seemingly minor exemption in copyright law could have large commercial implications for companies employing AI.

The chapter locates its analysis with a case study of Hong Kong, a city that depends on trade flows for its continued growth and development. Hong Kong also aims to be a leading smart city, but to date has only introduced regulations concerning data and external data flows on an uncoordinated and piecemeal basis. The chapter begins with a short historical overview of Hong Kong's quest to be a smart city and measures its progress against an objective. The chapter will then evaluate the potential downsides of Hong Kong's laissez-faire approach to regulation and advocate for the establishment of a coordinated framework and policy for managing cross-border data flows.

5.2 Hong Kong's Desire to Be a Smart City

Hong Kong has been formulating plans to become a leading global smart city and a leading innovation center for well over half a decade (Legislative Council 2016). For instance, in its ambitious *Hong Kong Smart City Blueprint* document released in December 2017, the Hong Kong government set out 76 initiatives under six smart areas—"Smart Mobility," "Smart Living," "Smart Environment," "Smart People," "Smart Government," and "Smart Economy" (Information and Technology Bureau 2017). A 2020 update to the 2017 Smart City Blueprint presented impressive statistics and accomplishments, including various infrastructure projects and other major initiatives that had been implemented in the past three years. Such measures included the Faster Payment System, free public Wi-Fi hotspots, and an "iAM Smart" one-stop personalized digital services platform (Information and Technology Bureau 2020). The government also announced investments in skills training such as science, technology, engineering, and mathematics (STEM) education and training on the application of technology for civil servants (Smart People Infographic, nd).

But a closer, detailed inspection of these documents reveals three omissions. First, neither Smart City Blueprint document includes a definition of "smart city." Second, aside from two mentions of the Law Tech fund and online dispute resolution, the two Blueprint documents pay scant attention to legal matters. (Information and Technology Bureau 2020) This lack of attention is a potentially serious future oversight given that the resolution of certain important questions of legal protection for data and databases are critical to the operation and development of AI systems. In fact, in its 2016 briefing to Hong Kong's legislature, the government only noted that the consultancy firm it hired for the smart city implementation (PricewaterhouseCoopers Advisory Services Limited 2017) would study the legal framework and experiences in other cities/countries and relevant overseas experiences "conducive to the implementation of smart city initiatives, and identify legislative proposals, if needed, for underpinning smart city development" (Legislative Council 2016, p. 5). Finally, despite their obvious importance to the ongoing operation of many of the initiatives mentioned in the two documents—in particular items under the umbrella of a "Smart Economy"—there is no mention of a coherent policy regarding cross-border data flows.

Given the release of aspirational documents lacking detail and follow-up, how does Hong Kong rate as a "smart city"?

5.3   What Is a Smart City—And Is Hong Kong a Smart City?

The answer to this question is more difficult than one would imagine, as there is a lack of consistent definition for the term "smart city." Even leading tech companies define a smart city in differing ways, although the underlying reliance on data is clear, even if it is not expressly stated. For example, while Nvidia uses the definition of a smart city as "a place applying advanced technology to improve the quality of life for people who live in it" (Merritt 2020, para 7), Cisco defines a smart city as one that "uses digital technology to connect, protect, and enhance the lives of citizens. Internet of Things (IoT) sensors, video cameras, social media, and other inputs act as a nervous system, providing the city operator and citizens with constant feedback so they can make informed decisions" (Cisco, nd). Meanwhile, Technopedia states that a smart city is "one in which sensor-driven data collection and powerful analytics are used to automate and orchestrate a wide range of services in the interests of better performance, lower costs and lessened environmental impact" (Kottayil 2021).

While neither of Hong Kong's Smart City Blueprints defines a "smart city," a 2016 planning document entitled Hong Kong 2030+, A Smart, Green and Resilient City Strategy offers a definition adapted around the "Smart City Wheel" concept mentioned in a 2014 Boyd Cohen article, Fast Company, that mentions several pioneering smart cities such as Barcelona, Copenhagen, Vancouver, and Singapore—but not Hong Kong (Cohen 2014). The planning document states that "[c]onventionally, a 'smart city' refers to a city that utilises ICT to make its components, infrastructure, utilities and services more efficient and interactive with the people" (Planning Department 2016).

Cohen's exclusion of Hong Kong was perhaps unfair as when measured against that and the other criteria, Hong Kong qualifies as a smart city:

- 5G coverage now exceeds 90% (Government of Hong Kong 2021–22 budget 2021);
- Hong Kong has a smart airport with self-bag drops and smart check-in kiosks;
- Over 95% of its population use contactless Octopus smart cards to make payments;
- Mobile subscriber and household broadband penetration rates are nearly 284 and 94% respectively; and
- The data.gov.hk website boasts over 4180 unique data sets (Information and Technology Bureau 2020).

Moreover, in September 2018, Hong Kong's Monetary Authority launched the Faster Payment System to enable users of banks and stored value facilities to make instant cross-bank/e-wallet payments easily by entering the mobile phone number or the email address of the recipient (Office of the Government Chief Information Officer Innovation and Technology Bureau 2019) and the government is presently developing two InnoHK research clusters at the Hong Kong Science Park, one focusing on healthcare technologies and the other on artificial intelligence and robotics technologies, as well as a data technology hub and the Hong Kong-Shenzhen Innovation and Technology Park (Government of Hong Kong 2020–21 Budget Speech 2020).

Hong Kong has also embraced the notion that the concept of a smart city must extend beyond hardware and has accordingly invested in skills training and has a vibrant start-up community [with over 3360 start-ups employing 10,688 employees across 116 co-work spaces, incubators, and accelerators (StartmeupHK 2020)] In this regard, the planning document noted:

> A wider definition of "Smart city" extends from a purely technocentric concept to a concept that underpins urban performance in economic and social development.... a city is smart "when investments in human and social capital and traditional and modern communication infrastructure fuel sustainable economic growth and a high quality life, with wise management of natural resources; through participatory governance. (Planning Department 2016)

However, Hong Kong's implementation of smart city infrastructure has been uneven with some areas still struggling with subpar internet and mobile services (Newbery 2021). Small cracks in a city's framework are commonplace, however, and cannot solely be used to judge a smart city.

5.4 Can Hong Kong Remain a Smart City?

If we concede that Hong Kong is currently a smart city, the next question to ask is whether it can retain this status. Two interrelated concerns quickly spring to mind: a lack of a coordinated policy on cross-border data flows and potential legal shortcomings. Both are addressed in turn.

5.4.1 Hong Kong's Lack of a Coordinated Data Policy

Could Hong Kong's current lack of a coordinated data policy hinder its future growth prospects given the ubiquity of data and the dependence of modern, highly interconnected systems on data? If anything, Hong Kong's reliance on international data flows for international commerce and financial transactions, product development, and innovation will only increase. There are many reasons for this conclusion, including the continued growth of transactions conducted using central bank digital currencies and the introduction of new technological innovations such as non-fungible tokens (NFTs)–which raise several potential concerns including intellectual property (IP), securities, anti-money laundering, contractual, and criminal concerns as well as data flow issues.

For instance, a person buying NFT art buys a token and the work of art linked to it, thus the linked art, the associated block chain ledger, and payment systems are necessary components of the NFT, all of which require data access to the token and the growing reliance on AI (West and Allen 2018). In addition, Hong Kong's Monetary Authority is currently in discussions with the Digital Currency Institute, a research unit of the People's Bank of China (PBOC), to pilot test China's CBDC, the Digital Currency Electronic Payment (DCEP), which is part of the PBOC's ambitious project to develop a digital currency. The DCEP is important to Hong Kong because if implemented successfully and quickly, it would cement Hong Kong's position as the premiere Asian financial hub. Thus, it would be in Hong Kong's interest to ensure the smooth implementation of DCEP without any data flow related issues (Le 2020).

The interconnectedness of contemporary digital systems means that actions in one area may have unintended consequences elsewhere. For instance, in 2018 the UK's plans to impose a 2.5% tax on sales in social media platforms were promptly met with threats of American retaliation and dimmed prospects for a US–UK trade deal (Sherman 2018). Likewise, when Australia announced in early 2021 its intention to introduce laws forcing tech companies to pay for Australian news content (Mishra 2021), Google and Facebook immediately pushed back, with the former threatening to remove its search engine from Australia (Clayton 2021), the latter threatening to forbid Facebook and Instagram users from sharing local and international news (Meade 2020), though a resolution was eventually reached (Diaz and Bond 2021; Samios 2021). Meanwhile, European efforts to regulate the obligations of digital services that act as intermediaries in their role of connecting consumers with goods, services, and content and introduce rules for platforms that act as "gatekeepers" in the digital sector were met with resistance and accusations of being protectionist and discriminatory (Curi 2020). The above situation would tend to support the government's need to formulate a coordinating policy after consulting with multiple stakeholders if for no other reason to mitigate the risk of unintended consequences similar to what recently happened to other jurisdictions.

5.4.2 Legal Shortcomings

Unlike some other jurisdictions, Hong Kong does not have laws specifically addressing smart cities. Hong Kong does, however, have laws addressing relevant aspects of a smart city, including privacy in the form of the Personal Data (Privacy) Ordinance, Cap. 486 (PDPO), e-commerce with the Electronic Transactions Ordinance, Cap 553 and electronic surveillance with the Interception of Communications and Surveillance Ordinance, Cap. 589. However, parts of Hong Kong's laws may become problematic in the future, particularly for the development and deployment of AI given that much of contemporary AI is a combination of software and data—including (i) the input training, testing and operational datasets; (ii) that input data as processed by the computer; (iii) the output data from those processing operations; and (iv) insights and data derived from the output data that distinguish such systems from most other conventional applications (Kemp 2020) and present subtle but potentially significant legal, trade, and business implications. To understand this, we need to consider AI's relationship with data.

5.4.2.1   The Relationship Between AI and Data

Most modern AI relies on large amounts of input data, and thus data flows are a critical concern not just for training data purposes, but also to update or adapt products for local market conditions as well as conduct remote (and cross-border) technical meetings and other collaborative activities. AI developers may also need access to infrastructure and tools such as Facebook's PyTorch, Google's Tensorflow, Salesforce's Einstein, or other cloud-based tools while creators, marketers, and others involved in sales and marketing of AI and AI-powered products would need access to tools to create brochures and other sales material as well as social media sites to promote their products.

5.4.2.2   Why Data Curation Is Important

In creating the data sets to train AI systems, considerable resources may be spent finding suitable training data, collecting the data, correcting training errors, or ensuring the data has not been corrupted (for example, by a cyberattack). The effort spent in data curation, defined as the active and ongoing management of data through its lifecycle of interest and usefulness (Horowitz 2019), and building up the relevant databases and data sets, can be significant. To create data sets, AI developers can

- Use data in the public domain (though this option has risks of bias and data unsuitability) (Calo 2017);
- Purchase data;
- Attempt to use technology to build AI less reliant on large data sets—for example one-shot learning (Sucholutsky and Schonlau 2020) or data set distillation (Sucholutsky and Schonlau 2019), though these technologies are neither proven nor mature; or
- Generate the data themselves, for example, using a text and data mining (TDM) system; data mining is the process of finding styles and extracting useful statistics from large data sets. Text mining is an AI technology that entails processing facts from numerous textual content files (Tariq 2020).

5.4.3 The Importance of Clarifying the Legal Protections for Data

The important legal question is whether a Hong Kong company creating a data set can protect its data under Hong Kong law, notably the Copyright Ordinance (Cap. 528), particularly if it is using a TDM system. Internet protocol (IP) protections for data are limited in Hong Kong, privacy protections under Hong Kong's PDPO notwithstanding. While it is tempting to think that any collections of data used in AI as databases could be protected as literary works, this is not necessarily the case. As per s.4(1)(a) of Hong Kong's Copyright Ordinance, a literary work includes "a compilation of data or other material, in any form, which by reason of the selection or arrangement of its contents constitutes an intellectual creation, including but not limiting to a table." Whether such protection is available to any such data set is not entirely clear.

5.4.3.1 Is It a Database?

If, for example, a user employs a TDM that scrapes data from the web and copies this into an organized collection of structured information or data, that is, a "database" (Oracle 2021), it could receive protection under the Copyright Ordinance. But what if the TDM mechanically copies that data into an unstructured file? It is debatable whether such action would qualify as an "intellectual creation" eligible for legal protection as a literary work.

As Hong Kong statutory and case law lacks a more precise definition of what "a compilation that, by reason of the selection or arrangement of its contents, constitutes an intellectual creation" means, it is not clear to what minimum standard of "intellectual creation" a collection of data requires for protection. It is also unclear whether such a collection might somehow qualify as a "database" given that the Copyright Ordinance lacks this definition.

In comparison, other jurisdictions provide a clearer framework. For example, the relevant laws in the UK contain provisions for databases, which is defined in s3A(1) CDPA as collections of independent works, data, or other materials, which are arranged in a systematic or methodical way and are individually accessible by electronic or other means. Similarly, Europe grants copyright protection to databases, which, as such, by reason of the selection or arrangement of their contents, constitute the "author's own intellectual creation." In parallel to the copyright protection on the structure of the database, European Union (EU) Directive 96/9/EC of the European Parliament and of the Council of 11 March 1996 on the legal protection of databases offers additional *sui generis* protection to databases to reward the substantial investment of the database maker in creating the database and prevent freeriding on somebody else's investment in creating the database. (Debussche and César 2019). Meanwhile, the US protects databases under copyright law (17 U.S.C. § 101) as compilations that are defined as a "collection and assembling of pre-existing materials or of data that are selected in such a way that the resulting work as a whole constitutes an original work of authorship." The compilation of facts is copyrightable only if the selection or arrangement "possesses at least some minimal degree of creativity (see Feist Publications, Inc. v. Rural Telephone Service Co., 499 U.S. 340 [1991]).

5.4.3.2   What About Copyright in the Embedded Items?

Even if such a collection could qualify for legal protection under the Copyright Ordinance, there is the question of whether the individual items contained in the data collection individually retain copyright rights. For instance, a database of songs may contain pictures of artists, songs, or videos that each individually hold IP rights.

There is a real risk that the use of TDM systems may infringe on such rights (Rubinfeld and Gal 2016) and at the IP right holders could create barriers, thereby affecting, *inter alia,* the use of such data. This effect could impact new system development, business models, etc. as the protection of the database as a collection, or in the case of Hong Kong, a compilation that constitutes an intellectual creation, does not extend to the underlying data. This point was echoed in Article 10(2) of the World Trade Organization's Agreement on Trade Related-Aspects of Intellectual Property (TRIPS Agreement), which reads:

> Compilations of data or other material, whether in machine-readable or other form, which by reason of the selection or arrangement of their contents constitute intellectual creations shall be protected as such. Such protection, which shall not extend to the data or material itself shall be without prejudice to any copyright subsisting in the data or material.

Hong Kong's Copyright Ordinance lacks an explicit exemption for TDM, which could limit the utility of the data set for AI training, as only TDM tools that involve minimal copying of a few words or crawling through data and processing each item separately could be operated without potentially encountering a liability (Geiger et al. 2018) The only exception could perhaps be if TDM were involved in a statutory inquiry (s. 55) and incidental inclusion for incidental inclusion of copyright material in an artistic work, sound recording, film, broadcast, or cable programme (though not in a literary work) under s. 40(1) of that ordinance.

This situation is again unlike the UK, EU, and US, which provide a TDM exemption in the form of a right to make a copy of a work "for computational analysis of anything recorded in the work" under s.29A of the UK's CDPA, which permits copying for non-commercial research, as long as the copy is accompanied by a sufficient acknowledgement (unless this would be impossible for reasons of practicality or otherwise) but requires authorization from the copyright holder for other uses (Okediji 2016). There is also an exemption in the EU under Art. 3.1 Directive (EU) 2019/790 on copyright in the Digital Single Market which provides an exception for TDM for scientific research and applies a liberal regime of fair use, with courts having held that the use of large volumes of copyrighted literary work for machine mining falls within the fair use exception based on the fact that the data use did not provide an alternative version of the copyrighted literary work to the public, but only snippets of it (O'Malley 2020).

5.4.4 Should Hong Kong Introduce an Exemption?

Should Hong Kong amend its Copyright Ordinance to define databases and provide explicit TDM exemptions? Would doing this attract more tech investment or spur more innovation? Thus far, the lack of a TDM exemption has not become an issue, and overseas experience has not unequivocally demonstrated that modifications of laws result in changes to investments in innovation. For example, while some have claimed that the US's more permissive software patenting regime is a primary reason more software development took place in the US than the EU, when the US Supreme Court's decision in Alice Corp. v. CLS Bank International (573 U.S. 208 [2014]) made it harder to get patents for software, the US did not see an outflow of investment, innovation, or talent. Similarly, the European Commission's evaluation of the Database Directive noted that the enactment of the Directive did not result in any significant new flows of technological investment into the EU (European Commission 2018).

5.5 Options for Hong Kong?

Hong Kong could continue its present laissez-faire policy, though, as noted earlier, this (non-)strategy has risks. Hong Kong could also make some minor changes to the way it operates, for example, amending the Copyright Ordinance. But in this specific case, Hong Kong may not feel any need to rush updates to its Copyright Ordinance given that both the Berne Convention and the Trade-Related Aspects of Intellectual Property Rights (TRIPS) Agreement (to which Hong Kong as a member of the World Trade Organization [WTO] is a party) provide for exceptions to copyright infringement depending on the purposes of the use of an otherwise protected work. More specifically, Article 9(2) of the Berne Convention establishes three conditions for exceptions and limitations to the right of reproduction: (i) only in certain special cases; (ii) only if there is no conflict with a normal exploitation of works; and (iii) only if there is no unreasonable prejudice to the legitimate interests of authors. Article 13 of the TRIPS Agreement provides similar criteria.

A third option would be for Hong Kong to adopt a wait-and-see approach, relying on developments in international bodies such as World Intellectual Property Organization (WIPO) or the WTO before amending its laws. But such an approach could take a long time, as reform in these institutions is inevitably slow and uncertain. For instance, WIPO initiated a process on IP and AI in 2019, when it held multiple "Conversation on IP and AI" conference events, a public consultation in which it received over 250 submissions, a draft paper, (WIPO 2019) and an event on "Copyright in the Age of Artificial Intelligence," (Copyright.gov 2020) yet still has not reached any global consensus on TDM exemptions or other AI-related IP issues. Moreover, even when WIPO members can reach a consensus, a new treaty can take years to ratify. For instance, while the Marrakesh Treaty to Facilitate Access to Published Works by Visually Impaired Persons and Persons with Print Disabilities was signed on June 28, 2013, it only came into force on September 30, 2016 (WIPO Marrakesh Treaty).

Likewise, the WTO will not provide Hong Kong or any other jurisdiction with a legal framework to facilitate the transfer of data, outline the contours of AI, or resolve associated IP controversies. The WTO framework was created long before technological breakthroughs on AI—even before the advent of global e-commerce and the WTO's attempts to grapple with the challenge posed by socio-technological change have largely failed. In this regard, the Electronic Commerce Work Programme and potentially a plurilateral agreement on e-commerce remain under discussion and unresolved (Liu and Lin 2020). Moreover, while the TRIPS Agreement is comprehensive in scope and provides substantive obligations, it is in many respects a minimum standards agreement which provides scope for members to tailor their laws to meet their needs and priorities. Thus, all approaches outlined in this chapter are compliant with the TRIPS Agreement.

Certain WTO members have advanced the agenda by entering bilateral and regional trade agreements to deal with, *inter alia,* provisions on cross-border data flows and/or data localization. For example, the Comprehensive and Progressive Agreement for Trans-Pacific Partnership.

- Includes provisions requiring "the cross-border transfer of information" subject only to restrictive measures being taken for a "legitimate public policy purpose" so long as the restrictions are not discriminatory or disguised trade barriers;
- Mandates strong copyright protection and enforcement;
- Provides for non-discriminatory treatment of digital products;

- Prohibits localization requirements for computing facilities, with a public policy exception similar to the one for cross-border data flows and personal information protection;
- Bars the mandated transfer or access to source code of software owned by a person of another party "as a condition for the import, distribution, sale or use of such software, or of products containing such software, in its territory" as well forced technology transfers; and
- Prohibits customs duties on digital trade.

Following the negotiation of the CPTPP, similar hard rules on data flows were incorporated in numerous subsequent trade agreements, notably Singapore's bilateral trade agreements with provisions on cross-border data flows, such as the upgraded New Zealand–Singapore Closer Economic Partnership, the Australia–Singapore Digital Economy Agreement that entered into force in December 2020, and Sri Lanka–Singapore Free Trade Agreement 2018. Other examples include trade agreements between Chile–Uruguay (2016), Argentina–Chile (2017), Australia–Peru (2018) and Australia–Indonesia (2019) as well as the United States Mexico Canada Agreement, UK–Japan Comprehensive Economic Partnership Agreement and EU–UK Trade and Cooperation Agreement.

Here, Hong Kong has not let the lack of a coordinated policy framework stop it from negotiating provisions on cross-border data in its free trade agreements (FTAs). The most recent and comprehensive example of which is the Australia–Hong Kong Free Trade Agreement (AUHKFTA), which entered into force in January 2020. Chapter 11 of the AUHKFTA on e-commerce covers cross-border data and includes a dedicated e-commerce chapter, which is in line with the trends in modern FTAs. The chapter includes dedicated provisions on

- electronic signatures and electronic authentication;
- a legal framework governing electronic transactions consistent with the principles of the UNCITRAL Model Law on Electronic Commerce 1996 or the UN Convention on the Use of Electronic Communications in International Contracts 2005;
- consumer protection;
- prohibition of customs duties on electronic transmissions, including content transmitted electronically;
- freedom of movement of information, including financial services;
- ban on localization of computing facilities, including financial services;
- protection of personal information;
- paperless trading;
- unsolicited commercial electronic messages;
- prohibition on requiring transfer or access to source code; and
- cooperation on development, enforcement, and by other means.

Whether these provisions become codified in domestic law or form the basis of a coordinated and coherent policy framework remains undetermined.

What is clear is that while Hong Kong can attribute much of its present success to its laissez-faire business policy, given the complex interdependencies of cross-border data flows its continued adherence to a laissez-faire cross-border data flow policy is likely not sustainable in the light of new digital realities. To ensure its various internal departments better appreciate the importance of data flows in their respective areas of responsibility and oversight, interdepartmental discussions are needed, and these discussions should lead to some internal consensus or position on how Hong Kong can ensure it remains a smart city. The Hong Kong government should then provide for a broad consultation focusing on whether Hong Kong should have a policy on data flows given how important data is to a smart city. Given that such a policy could have profound cross-industry implications, and with the 2014 Digital 21 consultation (launched on September 18, 2013 and ending on November 30, 2013) as a guide, the government should grant adequate time to solicit views (Hong Kong Government Press Release 2013). As part of the consultation, the government should map out how it might want to introduce new initiatives that could impact data flows, such as imposing charges for local news content on search engines. The consultation should also consider assessment criteria, that is, how Hong Kong should assess the success of new programs or policies or how and how quickly it should withdraw failed or problematic initiatives. It is only through a comprehensive and holistic consultation and review that the government can best formulate policy and advance the agenda of ensuring Hong Kong can remain a smart city.

Acknowledgements The authors gratefully acknowledge funding by the Hong Kong Policy Innovation and Co-ordination Office's Public Policy Research Funding Scheme for a project entitled Regulating Cross-Border Data: A Public Policy Framework for Hong Kong (Project No. 2019.A4.064.19D).

References

Calo (2017) Artificial intelligence policy: a primer and roadmap. 51 UC Davis L Rev 399–435
Cisco (nd) What is a smart city? https://www.cisco.com/c/en/us/solutions/industries/smart-connec
    ted-communities/what-is-a-smart-city.html
Clayton J (2021) Google threatens to withdraw search engine from Australia. https://www.bbc.com/
    news/world-australia-55760673
Cohen B (2014) The smartest cities in the world. http://www.fastcoexist.com/3038765/fast-cities/
    the-smartest-cities-in-the-world
Copyright.gov (2020) Copyright in the age of artificial intelligence. https://www.copyright.gov/eve
    nts/artificial-intelligence/agenda.pdf
Curi M (2020) EU digital services, markets proposals prompt a U.S. industry backlash. Inside US
    trade, 16 Dec 2020. https://insidetrade.com/daily-news/eu-digital-services-markets-proposals-
    prompt-us-industry-backlash. See also: Digital Services Act—Questions and Answers, https://ec.
    europa.eu/commission/presscorner/detail/en/QANDA_20_2348; Digital Markets Act: Ensuring
    fair and open digital markets (europa.eu), https://ec.europa.eu/commission/presscorner/detail/en/
    QANDA_20_2349

Debussche, J, César J (2019) Big data, issues and opportunities: Intellectual property rights. https://www.twobirds.com/en/news/articles/2019/global/big-data-and-issues-and-opport unities-ip-rights

Diaz J, Bond S (2021) Facebook to restore news content after brokering deal with Australian regulators. https://www.npr.org/2021/02/23/970429807/facebook-restores-news-con tent-after-brokering-partial-deal-with-australian-regu

European Commission (2018) Evaluation of directive 96/9/EC on the legal protection of databases, Brussels 25.4.2018 (European Commission 2018B). https://ec.europa.eu/digital-single-market/ en/news/staff-working-document-and-executive-summary-evaluation-directive-969ec-legal-pro tection

Geiger et al (2018) Text and data mining in the proposed copyright reform: making the EU ready for an age of big data? 48 IIC—International Review of Intellectual Property and Competition Law (2018) July 5, 2018. https://ssrn.com/abstract=3260037

Government of Hong Kong (2020) The 2020–21 budget speech by the financial secretary, the Hon Paul MP Chan moving the second reading of the Appropriation Bill 2020 Wednesday, 26 February 2020. https://www.budget.gov.hk/2020/eng/pdf/e_budget_speech_2020-21.pdf

Government of Hong Kong (2021) The 2021–22 budget speech by the financial secretary, the Hon Paul MP Chan moving the second reading of the Appropriation Bill 2021 Wednesday, 24 February 2021. https://www.budget.gov.hk/2021/eng/pdf/e_budget_speech_2021-22.pdf

Hong Kong Government Press Release (2013) Government consults public on 2014 Digital 21 strategy. 18 Sept 2013. https://www.info.gov.hk/gia/general/201309/18/P201309180530.htm

Horowitz B (2019) Implementations of cyber attack: resilience solutions for cyber physical systems. In: Lawless W, Mittu R, Sofge D, Moskowitz IS, Russell S (eds) Artificial intelligence for the internet of everything. Academic Press, Massachusetts, pp 87–100

Information and Technology BureauInformation and Technology Bureau (2017) Hong Kong smart city blueprint. https://www.smartcity.gov.hk/modules/custom/custom_global_js_css/assets/files/ HongKongSmartCityBlueprint(EN).pdf

Information and Technology BureauInformation and Technology Bureau (2020) Hong Kong smart city blueprint 2.0. https://www.smartcity.gov.hk/modules/custom/custom_global_js_css/assets/ files/HKSmartCityBlueprint(ENG)v2.pdf

Kemp R (2020) Intellectual property in algorithms, computer generated works and computer imple- mented inventions. https://www.mondaq.com/uk/patent/952154/algo-ip-intellectual-property-in- algorithms-computer-generated-works-and-computer-implemented-inventions

Kottayil NK (2021) Smart city https://www.techopedia.com/definition/31494/smart-city

Le K (2020) Hong Kong may be first global 'sandbox' for China's DCEP digital yuan. https://for kast.news/hong-kong-pilot-test-china-dcep-digital-currency

Legislative Council (2016) Panel on information technology and broadcasting. Smart city develop- ment in Hong Kong LC Paper No. CB(4)1087/15-16(04). 13 Jun 2016. https://www.legco.gov. hk/yr15-16/english/panels/itb/papers/itb20160613cb4-1087-4-e.pdf

Liu H-W, Lin C-F (2020) Artificial intelligence and global trade governance: a pluralist agenda. Harvard Int Law J 61(2):407–450. https://ssrn.com/abstract=3675505

Meade A (2020) Facebook threatens to block Australians from sharing news in battle over landmark media law. https://www.theguardian.com/media/2020/sep/01/facebook-instagram-thr eatens-block-australians-sharing-news-landmark-accc-media-law

Mendoza R (2020) Switzerland president slams Facebook's Libra: the project has failed. https:// www.ibtimes.com/switzerland-president-slams-facebooks-libra-project-has-failed-2894855

Merritt R (2020) What is a smart city? How AI is going uptown around the globe. https://blogs.nvi dia.com/blog/2020/08/06/what-is-a-smart-city/

Mishra S (2021) Australia passes amended law to make Google and Facebook pay for news. https://www.independent.co.uk/news/world/australasia/australia-news-law-facebook-goo gle-b1807154.html

Newbery D (2021) Two years on, smart city Hong Kong is still out of reach for 'remote' Sai Kung village. https://www.scmp.com/comment/letters/article/3115931/two-years-smart-city-hong-kong-still-out-reach-remote-sai-kung

Okediji RL (2016) Government as owner of intellectual property? Considerations for public welfare in the era of big data. Vanderbilt J Entertainment Technol Law 18(2):331–362

O'Malley K (2020) WIPO conversation on intellectual property (IP) and artificial intelligence (AI) third session. https://www.wipo.int/edocs/mdocs/mdocs/en/wipo_ip_ai_3_ge_20/wipo_ip_ai_3_ge_20_inf_5.docx

Office of the Government Chief Information Officer Innovation and Technology Bureau (2019) Update on smart city development, LC Paper No. CB(1)876/18-19(03). 16 Apr 2019. https://www.legco.gov.hk/yr18-19/english/panels/itb/papers/itb20190416cb1-876-3-e.pdf

Oracle (2021) https://www.oracle.com/database/what-is-database/

Planning Department (2016) Hong Kong 2030+, a smart, green and resilient city strategy. https://www.hk2030plus.hk/document/Hong%20Kong%202030+%20A%20SGR%20City%20Strategy_Eng.pdf

PricewaterhouseCoopers Advisory Services Limited (2017) Office of the Government Chief Information Officer Innovation and Technology Bureau, 'Smart city Development, LC Paper No. CB(4)1344/16-17(02). https://www.legco.gov.hk/yr16-17/english/panels/itb/papers/itb20170710cb4-1344-2-e.pdf)

Rubinfeld DL, Gal M (2016) Access barriers to big data. Arizona Law Review 59:339

Samios Z (2021) Rupert Murdoch's news corp signs global news deal with Google. https://www.smh.com.au/business/companies/rupert-murdoch-s-news-corp-signs-global-news-partnership-deal-with-google-20210218-p573j6.html

Sherman N (2018) US attacks UK plan for digital services tax on tech giants. BBC News. https://www.bbc.com/news/business-46050724

Smart People Infographic (smartcity.gov.hk). https://www.smartcity.gov.hk/modules/custom/custom_global_js_css/assets/images/infographic/smart_people_infograh.pdf

StartupmeHK (2020) Hong Kong's Startup Ecosystem. https://www.startmeup.hk/about-us/hong-kongs-startup-ecosystem/

Sucholutsky I, Schonlau M (2019) Soft-label dataset distillation and text dataset distillation. https://arxiv.org/abs/1910.02551

Sucholutsky I, Schonlau M (2020) 'Less than one'-shot learning: learning N slasses from M<N samples. https://arxiv.org/abs/2009.08449

Tariq M (2020) Compare difference between text and data mining. http://www.aiobjectives.com/2020/10/14/compare-difference-between-data-mining-and-text-mining/

West DM, Allen JR (2018) How artificial intelligence is transforming the world. https://www.brookings.edu/research/how-artificial-intelligence-is-transforming-the-world/

WIPO Marrakesh Treaty. https://www.wipo.int/marrakesh_treaty/en/

WIPO (2019) Draft issues paper on intellectual property policy and artificial intelligence WIPO/IP/AI/2/GE/20/1. https://www.wipo.int/meetings/en/doc_details.jsp?doc_id=470053

Chapter 6
The Promise and Challenges of Privacy in Smart Cities: The Case of Phuket

Visakha Phusamruat

Abstract The aim of this chapter is to examine privacy and personal data-related issues arising from the smart city development. Based on recent smart city campaigns in Phuket involving closed-circuit television (CCTV) installation and digitally-tracking wristbands, the author finds that local actors' privacy perceptions and data processing practices substantially deviate from the privacy views and practices required by the Thai Personal Data Protection Act. This deviation will potentially result in the lack of actual implementation or inevitable forced changes to the local community life just to meet the new legal standard. The global–local tension created by norms brought by visitors from various cultural backgrounds and the local tradition makes finding a common ground far more difficult. The case demonstrates the limitations of current legal approaches to embracing diverse societal views and interests, while also paving the possibility of a new way to understand privacy in smart cities and integrate this knowledge into their universal design.

6.1 The Promises of Smart City

6.1.1 Thailand's Smart City Concept

Smart city generally refers to the application of technologies to facilitate developments in the urban landscape (Sánchez et al. 2019). Like other smart cities around the world, Thailand's smart city embraces technology to enable solutions to today's city problems. Thailand defines smart city as "a city that takes advantage of modern technology and innovation to increase the efficiency of the city service and management, reduce the cost and resource usage of the target city and citizen." It focuses on good design and participation of business and public sectors in urban

V. Phusamruat (✉)
Graduate School of Law, National Institute of Development Administration, Bangkok, Thailand
e-mail: visakha.phu@nida.ac.th

© The Author(s) 2022   65
T. Phan and D. Damian (eds.), *Smart Cities in Asia*, SpringerBriefs in Geography, https://doi.org/10.1007/978-981-19-1701-1_6

development, under the concept of a modern and livable city development, for people in the city to have a good quality of life and sustainable happiness (Office of Smart City Thailand 2019). For a developer's project to be approved as smart city, the project must invest in some digital urban infrastructure in a defined area, a secure city data storage system, and a sustainable management for service delivery in at least two of the following seven core themes: smart environment, smart people, smart governance, smart mobility, smart living, smart economy, and smart energy (Office of Smart City Thailand 2019). Each theme has specific metrics. For instance, indicators for a project aimed to deliver smart living services are installations of closed-circuit television (CCTV) cameras, sensors, and the development of a platform connected with Internet of Things (IoT) devices to deter crime and improve city hygiene (Office of Smart City Thailand 2021, p 14).

6.1.2 Livable and Sustainable City as a Context

The agenda set by Thailand's 12th four-year National Economic and Social Development Plan (2017–2021) to create livable cities and advance sustainable development goals provides a backdrop for smart city development (Office of Smart City Thailand 2019, p 2). The plan set an agenda for a socioeconomic transformation focused on the use of high-tech and innovative methods to increase exported products and services, values, and the country's competitiveness in foreign investment, often referred to as the Thailand 4.0 policy (Office of the National Economic and Social Development Board 2016, p 2). At the regional level, the 2018 Association of Southeast Asian Nations (ASEAN) Smart Cities Framework initiatives introduced by Singapore, a pioneering smart nation, represent a concerted effort to find a uniform concept and actions for advancing smart city development in the region (The ASEAN Secretariat 2019). According to the Framework, the strategic outcome of smart cities is to promote high quality of life, competitive economy, and sustainable environment. Among the total of 26 cities first nominated by ASEAN members in 2018, Phuket was chosen by Thailand as a pilot city, followed by Chiangmai and Chonburi (Centre for Liveable Cities Singapore 2018).

6.1.3 Legal Landscape on Personal Data and Privacy Protection

There are currently no specific regulations for technology and data processing in smart city initiatives. Relevant laws include the Electronic Transactions Act of 2011, the Personal Data Protection Act of 2019 (the Thai PDPA), the Cybersecurity Act of 2019, the Official Information Act of 1997, and the Computer Crimes Act of 2007.

Regarding personal data and privacy protection, the Thai PDPA, inspired by the European Union's General Data Protection Regulation (EU GDPR) (2016) model and other legislation, provides duties for those engaging in personal data processing activities and guarantee of personal rights to personal data. The provisions generally apply to private and public actors who collect, use, or disclose personal data. Unless exemptions have been provided, any processing of personal data in smart city projects must also comply with the PDPA specified requirements. These are, for instance, to inform and obtain consent from an individual, to have adequate security measures in place, to provide an individual with rights to access, and to rectify and delete personal data related to them. Due to the unpreparedness of firms impacted by COVID-19, key aspects of the PDPA, including data subject rights, have been exempted for specified business company categories in the amended Royal Decree (2021), which continues until May 31, 2022, save for data security responsibilities.

The smart city promotion government agency has also been working on a City Data Platform Development Guideline Draft to establish uniform practices for platform management (Office of Smart City Thailand 2017), but it contains only technical guides, such as the platform setup, fundamental protection provided for individual users. Despite the fact that one of the five strategic pillars for the success of smart cities is data security and privacy (Office of Smart City Thailand 2017), necessary legal safeguards against the abuse of technology and personal data are missing.

6.1.4 The Promises and Privacy Risks

While smart city developments have paved the way for the promising future of a modernized and livable city, the benefits received from data processing activities in smart city developments comes at the cost of increased individual vulnerability to growing threats to personal data and privacy. Insecurities arise as personal data entrusted to the city can potentially be used against a data subject without their knowledge or consensus, turning an individual into a "fixed, transparent, and predictable" target for government and commercial exploitation and bad actor attacks (Cohen 2013, p 1905).

In the next section, the author draws on the surveillance technology used to promote Phuket smart tourism campaigns to illustrate the local views and international practices related to privacy and personal data. Section 6.3 examines a variety of legal challenges presented by the Phuket case including (i) finding a common ground to the global–local privacy perception conflicts; (ii) new normality proposed by the Thai PDPA against the community view; (iii) unreasonable, unnecessary, and disproportionate data processing activities; and (iv) the lack of appropriate privacy-preserving legal mechanism. A consideration for integrating privacy into the city's architecture is proposed in Sect. 6.4, with a conclusion in Sect. 6.5.

6.2 The Case of Phuket Smart Tourism

This section illustrates the use of CCTV and wearable technology in smart tourism, the views of local governments and entrepreneurs, as well as international perspectives on the implications for privacy.

6.2.1 The Vision of Phuket Smart Tourism

Phuket, known as Andaman Pearl, is a 543-square-kilometer island in southern Thailand with a population of about 400,000 people and 8 million visitors each year. In pursuing a smart tourism goal, the island, positioning itself as a world-class tourist destination, aims to enhance visitors' and residents' experience by promoting trade and commercial activities with safer travel and easy access to landmarks and iconic tourist attractions (Centre for Liveable Cities Singapore 2018, p 51). The ultimate goals of smart tourism are to increase capacity to receive up to 13 million visitors, boost income and jobs in tourism, which account for 96.5% of the city's gross domestic product (GDP), and attract foreign investment to the city (Nanthaamornphong et al. 2020).

6.2.1.1 Public Places in Plain Sight

More than 1000 city-owned CCTVs are linked with those of private businesses to monitor public places such as parking lots, piers, and public boats to detect rule violation as part of the Phuket Eagle Eyes project, a safe city's campaign aimed at active crime prevention and making Phuket a safe tourist destination (Centre for Liveable Cities Singapore 2018, p 52). More free Wi-Fi hotspots, 5G highspeed internet, and additional cameras with facial recognition and automated license tracking are planned to connect and send information to the Phuket City Data Platform, where various types of analytics are undertaken by the city's partners in combination with analysis of data from public resources to learn about people's habits (Nanthaamornphong et al. 2020). Insights from the real-time data collected from CCTVs and electronic wristbands the government planned for the tourists will enable authorities to monitor activities on the island (Centre for Liveable Cities Singapore 2018, p 52). End users of the city data platform, such as entrepreneurs, will gain from utilizing insights and open data to find problems and to improve and innovate services (Samui Times 2018). The city administrator and the Thai Information and Communication Technology Department also benefit from accessing the platform's reports. Tourists and residents will receive news and event information from the official department and social media network and contact authorities in case of emergency through the platform (Software Industry Promotion Agency 2021).

6.2.1.2 Ao Por Smart Pier

The smart pier project was launched by the Digital Economy Promotion Agency (DEPA) in partnership with the pier operators to keep track of passenger numbers in each boat to avoid overcrowding, ensure their safety, and strengthen tourists' confidence following boat accident reports (National News Bureau of Thailand 2018, 2020). Ao Por Pier in Thalang district is a gateway for visitors to relax and enjoy the beauty of the neighboring islands, serving as a model for other piers. The renovation included automatic gates with smart card scanners and face recognition. Automated temperature screening devices were installed at the entrance. Ticketing kiosks gather personal information from all boat passengers, including tour operators, boat owners, captains, and crew members who must register themselves with an ID card and have their photos taken by the kiosks before their departure. Following registration, each person will receive a wristband with a quick response (QR) code feature designed specifically for sea activities (Manager Online 2020).

The pier operator and the government agency said the QR code could help locate passengers and save time and money on tracing, which can cost up to 5 million Thai baht for each person (Leesa-nguansuk 2021). According to the news article, the minister claimed that the wristband allows a tourist to access medical services from healthcare providers without having to carry any paperwork and to be expedited in the insurance claim process in case of incidents at sea (Tortermvasana 2020).

6.2.1.3 Digital Yacht Quarantine

Another wristband model, also known as a health tracker or smart watch, has become a highlight of Thailand's first digital yacht quarantine project. The trial in October 2020 was done by the DEPA in collaboration with an IoT network infrastructure provider, a wearable tech startup, a yacht marina safety operator, and the Thai Yacht Business Association (Tourism Authority of Thailand 2021). The campaign serves as an alternative state quarantine program for visa holders who choose to stay on a yacht rather than in hotels or the government-designated locations, and to ensure detection if they leave the permitted area. Visitors who participate in this program must wear the smart watch at all times during their 14-day onboard quarantine after receiving the COVID-swab test from medical personnel on shore and registering with the maritime safety operator. The smart watch's sensors can monitor the wearer's heart rate, blood pressure, body temperature, and location. Real-time data from the devices are displayed on the dashboard and matched with the wearer's profile, including age, gender, and country, enabling staff to monitor visitors' health and assess health risks during their 14 days. The system enables visitors to send an SOS signal if they need immediate assistance or to obtain advice when they become lost (Phuket Private All Tours 2021).

The campaign's aims are to maintain public health, bring back foreign visitors who made up about 60% of income in the yacht business, and revitalize the tourism industry suffering more than 320 million Thai Baht loss due to travel restrictions during the pandemic (Phuket News 2021; RYT9 2021). The marina safety operator was confident that this new standard would impress travelers in all areas, as the operator can also serve them with tourist information, emergency contact, insurance claims, and an e-payment service. Phuket has been chosen as a model followed by other smart cities for sustainable tourism management and a sandbox for city reopening with COVID-19 containment programs in Thailand (Kasemsuk 2021; Phuket News 2021; RYT9 2021).

6.2.2 The Government and Local Entrepreneurs' Privacy Perception

Even before the pandemic, tour operators, DEPA, Telecom, travel insurance companies, maritime safety providers, and the Tourism Authority of Thailand had planned smart wristbands for travelers as part of Phuket Smart Tourism. Smart wristbands were originally designed with location tracking, an e-wallet, and travel insurance in mind (Matichon 2020). According to reports in the media and the Smart City 2021 proposal, the government intends to require visitors to wear wristbands and use the Thailand Plus smartphone app, which will allow authorities to track and notice when the band is removed, with potential legal consequences for the visitor. Data collected from wearable devices will be combined with government data to ensure precision and better disease control (Matichon 2020; Software Industry Promotion Agency 2021). The ministry's continued endorsement of the city's and its partners' initiatives reflects what the government and business leaders see as good and sound practices in prioritizing public interest and increasing profits to the economy as a whole, as well as claiming consumer convenience and better personal safety above fundamental privacy. The research, however, highlighted personal data protection rules as potential roadblocks to the implementation of the integrated CCTV cameras project and smart tourism project work, but stated that it will be safe based on individual consents received (Huawei Technology White Paper 2019, p 95).

6.2.3 Review of International Perspectives on Surveillance Technology

Many cities are considering banning pervasive surveillance technology to protect people's privacy. The Commercial Facial Recognition Privacy Act (2019) was in effect in San Francisco, a technological hub and a center of civil liberties advocacy, to restrict facial recognition and other remote biometric monitoring devices. The reasons for the restriction are to alleviate concerns about empowering the government tracking people in their daily lives and danger caused by technology.

In Hangzhou, East China's Zhejiang Province aiming to be the country's best digital governance, a draft bill was proposed to the local assembly in December 2020 to prohibit collecting biometric data without consent in residential communities. With rising threats from data leakage, identity theft, and personal privacy breaches, the residents fear biometric data and sensitive information such as the time and length they spend at home being disclosed to others. Therefore, many residents have refused to have their face information collected by the communities, despite some inconvenience caused by not sharing data (Lanlan 2020). In the EU where the GDPR is in effect, a municipality in Sweden has been fined for testing CCTV by monitoring the attendance of a class of students at school. The Swedish data protection authority found the school board failed to adequately assess risks to data subjects from sensitive biometric data processing, and that consent from an obviously weaker party alone may not be sufficient to give a lawful basis for the processing (European Data Protection Board 2019). The Dutch municipality's installation of sensors in shopping streets that can detect a Wi-Fi signal sent from a passerby's mobile phone for the purpose of counting the number of people was found to be unnecessary for the purposes of measuring the city center's crowdedness, and therefore it violated shoppers' and workers' privacy and their right to not being spied on as they go about their activities (European Data Protection Board 2021).

The international responses to the use of surveillance technology and risks to community life have clearly shifted toward the preservation of personal privacy, although certain technological gains in crime prevention and personal convenience must be sacrificed. Phuket can learn from other communities about their concerns and expectations around facial recognition technology and other monitoring equipment, as well as informed choices required for individuals to ensure that the processing of their personal data is not done without their knowledge or agreement. Essentially, when it comes to vulnerable targeted groups, consent alone may not be sufficient to justify the legitimate goals sought by the processing. Phuket city's council should consider listening to the residents' voices after educating them on the privacy impacts while following the worldwide trends to limit the use of biometric data, so that the user's travel experience design may properly take into account international tourists' and Phuket's inhabitants' true concerns.

6.3 Challenges for Privacy and Personal Data Protection from Phuket Experience

6.3.1 Finding a Common Ground for Global–Local Privacy Expectation

The evident contrast between the Thai appropriate practices of personal data and privacy perceptions and the recognized practices of enterprise and worldwide communities has raised the question of what constitutes a proper baseline for regulating activities in the public domain. While a study on privacy expectations of tourists and city residents using public areas is necessary to adequately assess the impact of personal data related processing activities proposed by smart city campaigns, the author opines that the intended use of the space by groups of users will help determine the level of privacy protection required. In the instance of the digital yacht quarantine, it would make more sense to create a default rule based on the higher expectations of international yacht tourists and the exclusive nature of this type of tourist. By contrast, since the piers are designated to be an immersive space for people of all cultures and backgrounds, from everyday ferry users to domestic and international visitors, options for the least intrusive means of personal data processing that caters to diverse individual preferences would reduce the discomfort experienced by people with high sensitivities. Care must also be exercised if different conditions are imposed for local and international visitors in order to avoid unfair and discriminatory treatment, particularly if a privacy choice comes at a higher cost of services.

6.3.2 The PDPA's Proposed New Normality and the Community Way

The fact that the local tradition differs greatly from the new Thai PDPA norms and globally recognized standards of practice has increased the possibility of non-compliance as well as negative feedback from tourists who are treated with superior legal protection in their home country. Changes made to comply with global norms, on the other hand, require unavoidable adjustments in people's engagement in community life. The locals may be compelled to be more reserved. What appears to be commonplace may be found unreasonable and prohibited under the new personal data protection regulations, for example, photographing and sharing a photo of people on the beach without their knowledge, public area surveillance by CCTVs, or private surveillance by a car owner's onboard camera device that records a view on the street and from a passenger's seat for accidental insurance claims.

6.3.3 Unreasonable, Unnecessary, and Disproportionate Data Processing Activities

The author found that current designs of processing activities may fail to adhere to reasonable personal information practices pursued by most jurisdictions.

As for the smart pier projects, the design of a smart wristband for boat passengers must follow the purpose specification and data minimization principles by collecting only the personal data necessary for protecting personal safety of the passenger at sea and for tracing after an accident. The continued tracking and recording of location data for all age groups during sea trips lasting from a half to a full day, without clear limits on who can access and on the retention period of personal data will fail the necessity requirement for protecting the pier operator's legitimate interest. Instead, the design should allow tracking and alerts only from a user's activation or when an incident occurs. A high volume of sensitive passenger registration data acquired from kiosks, including biometric data and the national ID card and password, exceeds what is required for counting people and preventing overcrowding on the boat. As alternatives for visitors, a less intrusive method that reveals fewer personal facts when a passenger gets onboard should be made available. If passengers do not have a choice to opt out of the insurance and health packages based on tracking, there is a risk that the negative impact on their privacy is not balanced by the benefits obtained by the data controller from processing the claims, given the unlikelihood of sea incidents and the availability of less intrusive means to ensure safety.

As for the case of digital yacht quarantine, the collection and sharing of health data like body temperature and COVID-like symptoms with officers is necessary for protecting personal vital interests and the public health as required by the quarantine mandate. Twenty-four-hour temperature and heart rate monitoring are, however, clearly unnecessary for ensuring compliance with the quarantine rule and unnecessary for persons who do not require intensive health checks. Sharing comprehensive health records and personal profiles with pier operator personnel in the same way as medical staff do is unnecessary processing. The vast scope and breadth of health data collected in real-time, 24 h a day for 14 days, obviously fall short of necessity and does not meet the proportionality balance required for compliance with quarantine rules. The case also implies that continuing to employ such wristband health tracking capabilities once the pandemic state improves will no longer justify the privacy impacts.

6.3.4   Absence of an Appropriate Tool for Privacy-Preserving Legal Mechanism

Specific protections such as the GDPR's obligation to conduct data protection impact assessments (DPIA) and the right to object to automated processing, as well as non-discrimination principles similar to the California Consumer Privacy Act 2018 (CCPA), are missing from the Thai PDPA and the guideline for smart city. According to the GDPR Art. 22, 35 and Recital 35, privacy high-risk practices, such as automated decision-making and profiling and mass surveillance in public places, require a data controller to conduct a DPIA to ensure that all threats have been thoroughly evaluated and appropriate measures to minimize the impact on individuals have been implemented before the processing begins. Non-discrimination protections under the CCPA Section 1798.125 strengthen a consumer's right not to sell their personal data and ensure that they will not be exposed to unjust discrimination or undue pressure from lower quality services or price increases. They also require businesses to explain the logic behind automated decisions, as well as any special offers or discounts offered to data subjects in exchange for benefits obtained by the use of their personal data. Phuket Smart City policy should be tailored to incorporate these privacy-preserving functions.

6.4 Moving Forward

6.4.1 Privacy in a Human City

Even though privacy aspects vary in each society, social values of privacy preserve trust, sincerity, and the confidence one needs in developing interpersonal relationships (Moore 2003, p 22; Richards and Hartzog 2016). Even from the standpoint of a non-individualist culture, privacy is essential since its loss causes personal insecurity and social instability (Lü 2020, p 7). In tourism, the self-discovery process allowed by the sense of freedom, autonomy, and authenticity experienced by a person or a group is made possible through privacy. Ning (2017) argues that authentic experiences involving personal and intersubjective feelings emerge from the existential state of being of a visitor when she expresses herself free of the constraints experienced in daily life. Privacy primarily functions as a safe space for emotional release, freedom from unwanted interference, for learning to develop one's personality, and define boundaries in relationships with others (Westin 1967). Privacy values therefore must be reintegrated into smart city measures in order to safeguard human capabilities to experience authenticity, set limits, and develop discernment on the values and information in front of them.

6.4.2 Universal Regulatory Design Considerations

A smart city regulation design should be adaptable, with a default set on a gradient scale and customization options to accommodate a wide range of privacy preferences of visitors and residents. When a privacy policy governing a place change, such as when entering a residential area with a high density of CCTVs, visitors should be prompted with a visual sign or cue to be informed. Designing a smart city regulation based on user experience can grasp privacy harm the laws of some jurisdictions have not yet recognized. For instance, the loss of ability to control their exposure to an environment and harms from surveillance as experienced by individuals from active means of categorizing, narrating, and norming in addition to being observed (Cohen 2008, p 194) can be addressed through a regulatory design that takes into account privacy impacts from real user experience. A tailored policy based on user experience can avoid dissonance and ideological conflicts between law in books and on the ground and increase regulatory soundness. With these privacy design considerations in mind, a city can demonstrate its openness to new digital culture by enhancing tourists' smart experiences at their own pace and achieve the smart city's goal.

6.5 Conclusion

The city's design of personal privacy safeguards matters because it affects the way a visitor experiences the city—how they learn about, connect with the people and the place, define the boundaries, and ultimately develop personal meanings from the city exploration process. Without adequate privacy protection, such freedom and autonomy are endangered by the data processing activities that have been made without one's knowledge, consent, willingness, or alternative choices available, thus interfering with one's decisional privacy. Threats to personal authenticity and freedom from misuse of technology can occur through an exposure of excessive monitoring of personal behaviors in people's private and leisure moments, which has led to the alteration of behaviors in personal interactions and self-censorship of some deviating behaviors. Proposed use of smart wristbands and other surveillance technologies in Phuket tourism campaigns, smart pier and digital yacht quarantine, demonstrates that local privacy perceptions vary significantly from the international perspectives provided by laws protecting personal data. The use of wristbands also raises questions about privacy risks, the reasonableness of the ongoing processing activities under the relevant laws, and the lack of adequate regulations to protect personal data and privacy in the smart city.

References

Laws, acts, and regulations referred to in the text

California Consumer Privacy Act (2018) Cal Civ Code, s. 1798.100-1798.199.100
Commercial Facial Recognition Privacy Act (2019) s.847 - 116th Congress 2019–2020
EU General Data Protection Regulation (GDPR): Regulation (EU) 2016/679 of the European parliament and of the council 2016
Personal Data Protection Act B.E. 2562 (2019) Thai Government Gazette, vol. 136, Chapter 69, (Gor) 2019
The Royal Decree Specifying Departments and Businesses Exempt from The Personal Data Protection Act B.E. 2562 (No.2) B.E. 2564 (2021), Thai royal gazette, Vol. 138, s. 32 (Gor)

Other sources

ASEAN Secretariat (2019) Association of south east Asian nation. Concept note: ASEAN smart cities framework, Jakarta. https://asean.org/storage/2019/02/ASCN-Concept-Note.pdf. Accessed 31 May 2021

Centre for Liveable Cities (2018) ASEAN smart cities framework. Ministry of National Development, Singapore. https://www.clc.gov.sg/docs/default-source/books/book-asean-smart-cities-network.pdf. Accessed 31 May 2021

Cohen JE (2008) Privacy, visibility, transparency, and exposure. U Chi L Rev 75(1):181–201

Cohen JE (2013) What privacy is for. Harv L Rev 126(7):1904–1933

European Data Protection Board (2019) Facial recognition in school renders Sweden's first GDPR fine. Press release. https://edpb.europa.eu/news/national-news/2019/facial-recognition-school-renders-swedens-first-gdpr-fine_en. Accessed 31 May 2021

European Data Protection Board (2021) Dutch DPA fines municipality for Wi-Fi tracking. Press release. https://edpb.europa.eu/news/national-news/2021/dutch-dpa-fines-municipality-wi-fi-tracking_en. Accessed 31 May 2021

Huawei Technology (2019) Smart city framework and guidance for Thailand: แผนการพัฒนาภูเก็ต. White paper, Thailand. https://e.huawei.com/th/material/local/c0c15fc0f8df4bb09a7bad4a246a9d72. Accessed 31 May 2021

Kasemsuk N (2021) Phuket reopening up for discussion. Bangkok Post. https://www.bangkokpost.com/business/2079147/phuket-reopening-up-for-discussion. Accessed 20 July 2021

Lanlan H (2020) Global times. China society, facial recognition systems boycotted at some Chinese cities' residential communities. https://www.globaltimes.cn/page/202012/1211356.shtml. Accessed 31 May 2021

Leesa-nguansuk S (2021) Smart wristbands for yacht tourists. Bangkok Post. https://www.bangkokpost.com/business/2080359/smart-wristbands-for-yacht-tourists. Accessed 31 May 2021

Lü YH (2020) Privacy and data privacy issues in contemporary China. In: Miller KW, Taddeo M (eds) The ethics of information technologies, vol 7. Routledge, London, pp 7–15

Manager Online (2020) Digital economy and society minister's first smart pier demo to boost confidence of tourists and residents. https://mgronline.com/onlinesection/detail/9630000113273. Accessed 31 May 2021

Matichon Online (2020b) MDES minister following-up visit on smart pier in support of COVID-free city reopening. Accessed 31 May 2021

Moore AD (2003) Privacy: Its meaning and value. APQ 40(3):215–227

Nanthaamornphong A et al (2020) A case study: Phuket city data platform. In: 2020 17th international conference on electrical engineering/electronics, computer, telecommunications and information technology (ECTI-CON), pp 717–722. https://doi.org/10.1109/ECTI-CON49241.2020

National News Bureau of Thailand (2018) Command visits Ao Po port in Phuket. Thainews. https://thainews.prd.go.th/th/news/detail/WNRGN6107300010001. Accessed 31 May 2021

National News Bureau of Thailand (2020) Phuket province, MDES smart pier showcases for COVID-19 free city reopening. https://thainews.prd.go.th/th/news/detail/TCATG201101202545169. Accessed 31 May 2021

Ning W (2017) Rethinking authenticity in tourism experience. In: Timothy DJ (ed) The political nature of cultural heritage and tourism: Critical essays, vol. 3 ,1st ed. Routledge, London, pp 469–490. https://doi.org/10.4324/9781315237749

Office of the National Economic and Social Development Board (2016) A summary of the twelfth national economic and social development plan (2017–2021), Bangkok. https://www.nesdc.go.th/ewt_dl_link.php?nid=9640. Accessed 20 July 2021

Office of Smart City Thailand (2017) City data platform development guideline 2017 draft, Bangkok https://drive.google.com/file/d/1rqp6IWNskg2XO0rTiEoYBWVtpXJPo26y/view?usp=sharing

Office of Smart City Thailand (2019) Smart city development steering committee announcement No. 1/2562 (2019) Re: Evaluation criteria, qualifications, means and procedure for designation of smart city. https://www.depa.or.th/storage/app/media/file/Smart%20City%201-2562-02-final.pdf. Accessed 20 July 2021

Office of Smart City Thailand (2021) Revised draft of the criteria of smart city project, Bangkok, https://drive.google.com/file/d/1Br94GHvO3tIZ0PVgP9LppUNEJObIzn06/view

Phuket News (2021) Phuket yacht visitors first to receive smart wristband trackers. https://www.thephuketnews.com/phuket-yacht-visitors-first-to-receive-smart-wristband-trackers-79284.php. Accessed 31 May 2021

Phuket Private All Tours (2021) The Thai yachting business association representative interview. online video. Facebook page. https://www.facebook.com/PhuketPrivateAllTours/videos/3832647893471747. Accessed 14 April 2021

Richards N, Hartzog W (2016) Taking trust seriously in privacy law. Stan Tech L Rev 19(3): 431–472

RYT9 (2021) DEPA joins AIS and Phuket network to revive tourism in the pearl of the Andaman launching new method of digital yacht quarantine. https://www.ryt9.com/en/prg/248218. Accessed 31 May 2021

Samui Times (2018) Thai govt plans to make foreign tourists in Phuket wear electronic wristbands. Thailand News. https://www.samuitimes.com/thai-govt-plans-to-make-foreign-tourists-in-phuket-wear-electronic-wristbands/. Accessed 20 July 2021

Sánchez CR et al (2019) Smart cities survey: Technologies, application domains and challenges for the cities of the future. Int J Distrib Sens Netw. https://doi.org/10.1177/1550147719853984

Software Industry Promotion Agency (2021) Phuket smart city. Online presentation. Phuket Province. https://www.phuket.go.th/webpk/file_data/smartcity/01.pdf. Accessed 31 May 2021

Tortermvasana K (2020) Bangkok Post. Ao Por pioneers smart pier mode. https://www.bangkokpost.com/business/2012919/ao-por-pioneers-smart-pier-mode. Accessed 31 May 2021

Tourism Authority of Thailand (2021) Phuket launches Thailand's first 'digital yacht quarantine' project. https://www.tatnews.org/2021/03/phuket-launches-thailands-first-digital-yacht-quarantine-project. Accessed 31 May 2021

Westin AF (1967) Privacy and freedom. Atheneum, New York

Chapter 7
The Emerging Legal Framework for Smart Cities in Vietnam

Nguyen Van Cuong

Abstract The idea of the "smart city" is widely understood in Vietnam today. On 1 August 2018, the prime minister issued a decision to approve a national plan for development of smart sustainable cities during 2018–2025, with a vision toward 2030. This decision sets a target to turn the four biggest cities in Vietnam (Hanoi, Ho Chi Minh City, Da Nang, and Can Tho) into cities with core smart functions by 2025 or 2030. However, most of the smart city projects remain at the pilot stage. There are several legal issues to be addressed to help those projects run smoothly. This paper traces the evolution of the legal framework for smart cities in Vietnam in recent years and the driving forces behind this evolution. It shows that the legal framework for smart city projects in Vietnam is still in an early stage of development with room for improvement, especially in the areas of legal rules for information and communication technology (ICT) application (especially digital signatures), urban governance of infrastructure, construction and engineering laws, intellectual property rights, and protection of personal data (data rights law and privacy law).

7.1 Overview on Urbanization in Vietnam

Urban areas, especially cities, play an important role in the promotion of economic, cultural, education, and social development. In 2014, the total human population living in cities accounted for about 54% of the global population, while this number in 1950 was only about 30%. It is expected that in 2050, 70% of the global population will be living in cities (Gassmann et al. 2019, p 6).

The number of Vietnamese citizens living in cities is much lower than in the rest of the world. Before 1990, especially before the launching of the "Doi Moi" (renovation) policy in 1986, urbanization was very slow in Vietnam but has sped up since the 1990s. In 1990, only 19.51% of the Vietnamese population resided in urban areas; this number stood at 36.82% in 2020 (GSO 2021, p 54). There are currently

N. Van Cuong (✉)
General Director, Institute of Legal Studies, Ministry of Justice of Vietnam, Hanoi, Vietnam
e-mail: Cuongnv@moj.gov.vn

© The Author(s) 2022
T. Phan and D. Damian (eds.), *Smart Cities in Asia*, SpringerBriefs in Geography,
https://doi.org/10.1007/978-981-19-1701-1_7

862 urban areas in Vietnam (including five centrally run cities,[1] 79 provincially-run cities, 51 towns, four districts, and 719 townships). These urban areas account for about 70% of Gross Domestic Product (GDP) in Vietnam (Tuan 2020).

Cities are often associated with good things, such as a wide range of economic opportunities and high quality of life. Cities are also associated with their negative aspects, such as crime, energy shortages, problems with garbage disposal and water supply and treatment, air pollution, noise, healthcare problems, high population density, social conflicts, overloading of infrastructure, and traffic issues (Gassmann et al. 2019, p 3). Urban areas are also vulnerable to pandemics like COVID-19. In Vietnam, like other cities, similar concerns are found, especially garbage collection and treatment, water supply and treatment, air pollution, noise, low-quality infrastructure, and traffic jams. It seems that urban managers face more and more pressures.

7.2 Definitions of Smart City

To make cities run smoothly and increase quality of life for their residents with more accessible public services, urban managers in many countries are now using a "smart city" model as an important solution to their daily problems. According to the International Standard Organization (ISO), a smart city is "a new concept and a new model, which applies the new generation of information technologies, such as the internet of things [IoT], cloud computing, big data and space/geographical information integration, to facilitate the planning, construction, management and smart services of cities" (Anthopoulos 2017, p 8). The International Telecommunication Union (ITU) also introduced a definition of "smart city" (with the term "smart sustainable city") in 2016. According to ITU, a smart city is "an innovative city that uses ICTs[2] and other means to improve quality of life, efficiency of urban operation and services, and competitiveness, while ensuring that it meets the needs of present and future generations with respect to economic, social, environmental as well as cultural aspects" (ITU 2016).

The Association of Southeast Asian Nations (ASEAN) Smart Cities Framework (adopted by ASEAN Smart Cities Network on 8 July 2018) states that.

> a smart city in ASEAN harnesses technological and digital solutions as well as innovative non-technological means to address urban challenges, continuously improving people's lives and creating new opportunities. A smart city is also equivalent to a "smart sustainable city", promoting economic and social development alongside environmental protection through effective mechanisms to meet the current and future challenges of its people, while leaving no one behind. As a city's nature remains an important foundation of its economic development and competitive advantage, smart city development should also be designed in accordance with its natural characteristics and potentials. (ASEAN 2018)

---

[1] Hanoi, Ho Chi Minh city, Hai Phong, Da Nang, and Can Tho.
[2] Information and communication technologies.

In a smart city, digital technologies and other advanced technologies[3] are systematically applied "to reduce resource input, improve its people's quality of life, and increase the competitiveness of the regional economy in a sustainable manner. It entails the use of intelligent solutions for infrastructure, energy, housing, mobility, services, and security, based on integrated sensor technology, connectivity, data analytics, and independently functional value-added processes" (Gassmann et al. 2019, p 25). Each smart city has six key dimensions: (1) smart environment,[4] (2) smart living,[5] (3) smart economy,[6] (4) smart mobility,[7] (5) smart government or governance,[8] and (6) smart people.[9] For more detailed guidance to implement smart city projects, the ISO has introduced a number of standards related to "smart cities," such as ISO 37120 "Sustainable development of communities—Indicators for city services and quality of life" (first introduced in 2014 and revised in 2018) (ISO 2018). This standard defines 21 city themes of city services and quality of life: (1) economy, (2) education, (3) energy, (4) environment and climate change, (5) finance, (6) fire and emergency response, (7) governance, (8) health, (9) housing, (10) population and social conditions, (11) recreation, (12) safety, (13) solid waste, (14) sport and culture, (15) telecommunications, (16) urban planning, (17) transportation, (18) urban/local agriculture and food security, (19) urban planning, (20) waste water, and (21) water.

In Vietnam, no official definitions of smart city exist in any laws enacted by the national assembly. However, in one guideline issued by the ministry of information and communication[10] in 2019, "smart sustainable city" is defined as "an innovative city that uses ICTs and other means to improve quality of life, efficiency of urban operation and services, and competitiveness, while ensuring that it meets the needs of present and future generations with respect to economic, social, environmental as well as cultural aspects." This definition is explicitly a copy of a definition of "smart sustainable city" in Recommendation ITU-T Y. 4900 by ITU as mentioned earlier.

---

[3] Such as sensors, CCTV, Internet of Things (IoT), artificial intelligence (AI), machine learning, super automation, machine to machine communication, "smart" energy grids, talking and serviceable "bots," driverless transport, advanced cybersecurity, and human–machine interface.

[4] This dimension includes efficient energy systems, green spaces, less extreme climate, reduced pollution, resource management, and smart management of solid waste and water waste.

[5] This dimension includes high quality of life composed of good health (availability of smart healthcare systems, smart sport activities, etc.), housing, culture, tourism, and safety.

[6] This dimension represents the economic competitiveness of the city including entrepreneurship, innovation, flexibility, the productivity of the labour market, trademarks, and participation in the global market.

[7] This dimension includes local and global accessibility with the presence of ICTs and sustainable, safe, convenient transport systems.

[8] This dimension includes an effective, efficient, and responsive government with active and well-informed participation of the people in the city based on ICTs and digital technologies.

[9] This dimension is concerned with the high level of qualification or education received by citizens and active participation of citizens in community activities. Citizens are the true authors of the community life in the city.

[10] Decision No. 829/QĐ-BTTTT dated 31 May 2019 by minister of information and communication of Vietnam issued "The ICT Reference Framework for development of smart cities (Version 1.0).".

This definition can be said to be the only official definition available at present in Vietnam.

7.3 Implementation of Smart Cities in Vietnam

The idea of the "smart city" is widely understood today in Vietnam. The term "smart city" was officially introduced into policies in Vietnam in 2016. Resolution No. 05/NQ-TW dated 1 November 2016 by the Communist Party's Central Committee, "on a number of major policies for renewal of the economic growth model, enhancing the quality of growth, labor productivity and national economic competitiveness," is perhaps the first resolution of the Communist Party of Vietnam in which the term "smart city" was used. This resolution has only one sentence dealing with smart cities: "priority should be set to turn some cities into smart cities." It does not explain what a smart city means. Following this step, on 1 August 2018, the prime minister of Vietnam issued Decision No. 950/QĐ-TTg approving the scheme for the development of smart sustainable cities in Vietnam in the period of 2018 to 2025 with orientations by 2030. The general objective of this scheme is.

> developing smart sustainable cities in Vietnam toward green growth and sustainable development by taking advantage of and promoting existing potentialities and strengths as well as enhancing the effective use of human resources; taking the best advantage of natural resources and human resources to improve the quality of life and facilitate organizations and individuals in studying and making the investment in construction and management of smart cities.

From 2018 to 2020, the scheme focused on the establishment of legal grounds for the development of smart cities and preparations for piloting smart city models in some urban areas and at least three cities. Also in this period, the scheme planned to formulate and pilot a smart city ICT reference framework; build spatial urban data infrastructure integrated with land data based on a Geographic Information System (GIS) database and others; develop appropriate models for managing population, transport, land, construction, and investments in pilot urban areas; and develop the national urban database. By 2025, the scheme will focus on the following activities: formulating and revising legal corridor and legislative documents based on preliminary and final reports on pilot smart cities; applying ICT reference framework to development of smart cities in Vietnam; announcing national standards serving pilot smart cities, giving priority for standards for urban management, lighting, traffic, water supply and drainage, waste collection and treatment systems, electrical grids, disaster and risk warning systems, and ICT infrastructure systems; developing spatial urban data infrastructure integrated with land and construction databases and others on the basis of GIS data in pilot cities; assisting at least six cities/six economic zones to obtain approval for master schemes for development of smart cities and developing smart city facilities serving residents in smart cities; establishing pilot citizen connect centers associated with single-window sections; and piloting the application of mechanisms for issuance of certifications of smart cities. By 2030, the scheme will gradually apply mechanisms and policies on a large scale according to sectors and regions and build a network of smart cities. According to the decision, this network of smart cities will be established "in the North of Vietnam, the Central part of Vietnam, the South of Vietnam, and Mekong Delta, in which Hanoi, Ho Chi Minh City, Da Nang, and Can Tho shall be nuclear cities, and establish linkages between smart cities." Unfortunately, Decision No. 950/QĐ-TTg does not have any definition of smart city or any set of criteria to classify an urban area as a smart city. To overcome this shortcoming, a definition of "smart sustainable city" has been stipulated in the Decision No. 829/QĐ-BTTTT dated 31 May 2019 by the minister of information and communication of Vietnam, issued as the "ICT Reference Framework for development of smart cities (Version 1.0)" as earlier mentioned. The Decision No.829/QĐ-BTTTT also sets forth key principles for development of smart cities in Vietnam as follows:

(a) Follow a people-centered approach;
(b) Ensure the ICT infrastructure capacity for creating a digital ecosystem that meets the development needs of apps and services for smart cities. Enhance the sharing of ICT infrastructure. Encourage open data including understandable data (clearly defined), use, and exploitation by all participants in construction of smart cities. Ensure open data owned by local governments and shared among stakeholders (if necessary);
(c) Ensure the neutrality of technology; paying due attention to ICT application suitable to smart cities, such as IoT, cloud computing, big data, AU, and those suitable to various platforms; make use of and optimize the existing ICT infrastructure;
(d) Ensure information safety and security, the capacity to respond to or handle information security incidents, especially for key information infrastructure; protect citizens' personal information;
(e) Ensure that smart city projects are consistent with current local planning and development strategies based on local reality and needs (such as need of management, citizens' needs, strengths, weaknesses, opportunities and challenges); inherit and sustainably develop local cultural, economic, social, material, and spiritual values;
(f) Set priority for overall missions or interdisciplinary tasks, such as ICT structure for smart cities, information safety, and broadband;
(g) Prefer reuse to purchase or new construction (applications or system elements should be reused if possible; purchase of goods should be considered only in necessary cases and new construction is selected only in cases where some requirements are impossible to be implemented);
(h) Manage data to ensure its correctness and to ensure quality of data is good enough for effective decision-making;
(i) Properly manage and share data (data for processing the same type of tasks of individuals, organizations or bodies shall be the same with a transparent origin);

(j)   Ensure accessibility of data (data shall be easily searched, inquired, and displayed as similar to authentic versions);

(k)   Pilot new services or applications (samples or experiments with users and improvement based on experience of users);

(l)   Use open standards or open sources (open standards are used for all solutions designed to enhance the interconnectivity; software with open source shall be examined or reviewed together with commercial software where technical solutions are selected).

In the national socio-economic development strategy of Vietnam for the period 2021–2030, Vietnam informs that it is projected to form a series of "smart cities" in the North of Vietnam, the Central part of Vietnam, and the South of Vietnam. These smart cities shall be gradually connected with a network of smart cities in the region (i.e., ASEAN) and the world (Communist Party of Vietnam 2021, p 260). It also specifically expresses the government's determination to turn Hanoi (the capital of Vietnam) into a "smart city" by 2030 that is modern, green, clean, beautiful, and safe (Communist Party of Vietnam 2021, p 254).

In practice, the number of provinces or centrally run cities interested in smart city projects to be implemented before the year of 2020 is far beyond the number (at least three cities) mentioned in Decision No. 950/QĐ-TTg. For example, on 23 November 2017, the People's Committee of Ho Chi Minh City issued Decision No. 6179/QD-UBND approving a grand project involving "Constructing Ho Chi Minh City toward a smart city for the period of 2017–2020, orientations by the year of 2025." This people-centered project focuses on accelerating the growth rate of the city's economy, improving effectiveness of city governance with better prediction, and an "active approach" rather than "passive replies," improving the living and working environment for the people and attracting more public participation to city governance. Some initiatives are mentioned in this grand project, such as high-quality public transportation with interconnected e-tickets, smart parking, open data for transportation systems, autonomous monitoring of traffic or construction violations, e-health dossiers, open data for healthcare services, open data for environmental problems, open data for education and job opportunities, e-administrative procedures, and an ecosystem for startups. This project also opens the door to set up a smart city steering center and a center for cybersecurity. Additionally, this project gives a green light to public–private partnership initiatives for delivering certain public city services.

Another example of smart city implementation is Bac Ninh Province,[11] which set up a "steering committee for smart city" in 2017. In September 2019, Bac Ninh completed a "pilot center for running the smart city" that hosts many databases including about 1100 statistical indicators in various sectors, such as education, healthcare, transportation, social affairs, finance, natural resources and environment, agriculture, technology and science, and public administration. This province also installed 286 CCTVs for monitoring traffic, which provided a useful tool for police to handle administrative violations or car accidents. In the next few years, about 3200

---

[11] A province in the north of Vietnam, about 30 km from the center of Hanoi.

CCTVs are expected to be set up for city governance (ST 2020). These CCTVs are directly connected to the "pilot center for running the smart city." By 2030, Bac Ninh expects it shall be governed under the model of a smart city.

Many other provinces and cities also follow the steps of these pioneers. On 9 March 2018, the People's Committee of Lao Cai Province issued a Plan No. 83/KH-UBND on deployment of construction of a smart city in Lao Cai Province for the period of 2018–2025. On 12 July 2018, Thua Thien—Hue Provincial Peoples' Council issued Resolution No. 12/NQ-HĐND ratifying the project on "Development of Smart City Services for Thua Thien—Hue Province up to 2020, orientations by the year of 2025" with a budget of 323 billion VND (equal to 14 million USD) for this project. On 29 December 2018, People's Committee of Da Nang City issued Decision No. 6439/QĐ-UBND ratifying the project on construction of a smart city in Da Nang City for the period of 2018–2025, orientations by the year 2030. On 1 August 2019, People's Committee of Yen Bai Province issued Decision No. 1373/QD-UBND approving the project to implement the smart city model in Yen Bai Province for the period of 2019–2021, orientations by the year 2025. On 12 December 2019, People's Council of Hai Duong Province issued a Resolution No. 20/2019/NQ-HĐND approving the project for construction of e-government and a smart city in Hai Duong Province for the period of 2020–2025, orientations by the year 2030.[12] On 28 February 2020, People's Committee of Nam Dinh Province issued a Plan No. 18/KH-UBND on deployment of smart city services in Nam Dinh Province. On 9 March 2020, People's Committee of Quang Ninh province issued Plan No. 47/KH-UBND on the development of smart cities in Quang Ninh Province for the period of 2020–2025, orientations by the year 2030.

It is interesting that the "smart city" has become such an attractive idea that not only big cities with good resources are interested in initiating their development, but some provinces in mountainous areas are also keen on such development. For example, Ha Giang Province (a mountainous province in the north) had a plan for its "smart city" in 2018 (to turn its central city, Ha Giang City, into a smart city). In accordance with Decision No. 2453/QĐ-UBND dated 2 November 2018 by the People's Committee of Ha Giang Province ratifying the smart city project applicable to Ha Giang City by the year 2020, the province invested 45 billion VND (i.e., about 2 million USD) for this project. This project focused on implementing a smart city application on smart phones (namely "MyCity") for all citizens of the city. With this application, citizens can easily access sources of city information (such as public service procedures, emergency information for health problems, fire and police services, and transportation information). With this application, citizens can send their opinions or reports to the city government directly. This project also enhances the digital transformation of planning processes, promotes smart tourism services (including provision of about 50 free Wi-Fi points in the city for tourists and citizens), sets up three autonomous environmental monitoring systems to control the city's air quality, and sets up a CCTV system for monitoring traffic jams and traffic violations. This project also provides a service of smart cards for students, for public servants,

---

[12] The budget for this project is 4,800 billion VND (equal to 210 million USD).

and for citizens and entrepreneurs to use their essential public services. Moreover, this project includes a "Smart City Operation Center" and a "Local Government Services Platform." In the south of Vietnam, Hau Giang Province (not yet a rich province), the provincial government also issued a Resolution No. 51/NQ-HĐND dated 4 December 2020 approving the project on e-government and smart city for 2021–2025 with a budget of 300.5 billion VND (equal to about 13 million USD). Perhaps urban managers hope smart city projects will contribute to the fast and sustainable long-term development of their cities and provinces.

So far, about 30 provincial governments or centrally run cities have formulated plans to implement smart city projects in their cities or provinces (Long 2021), including all five centrally run cities in Vietnam (Hanoi, Ho Chi Minh City, Da Nang, Hai Phong, and Can Tho). Other provinces have described their plans to carry out smart city projects in their provinces, for example, Thai Binh, Binh Thuan, Ba Ria—Vung Tau, Tien Giang, Gia Lai, and Binh Duong.

7.4   Emerging Legal Issues

To turn a traditional city into a smart one requires huge effort and various tasks.[13] For example, to make all transactions between local governments and their residents run smoothly online, digital signatures by local officials must be applied. Additionally, online payment methods must be accepted by local authorities in the provision of public services, such as registration of property, transactions, or business. Also, digital local governments require advanced cybersecurity technologies, a responsive and effective cybersecurity management system, as well as suitable penalties for cyberattacks. International experience shows that to implement a project to transform a traditional city into a smart city, besides finding appropriate ICT solutions, several concerns raised by the public and city managers must be considered, such as (1) securing sufficient funding to start and sustain the project, (2) overcoming citizen and business concerns over privacy and data sharing, and (3) aligning multiple city departments and stakeholders (Gassmann et al. 2019, pp 52–53).

To meet this demand, Vietnam has taken some steps to improve its legal system. For example, the Law on Cyber Information Safety of 2015 has certain provisions on protection of personal information. This law (Article 16) states that agencies, organizations, and individuals that process personal information shall ensure cyber information security for the information they process. Organizations and individuals that process personal information shall develop and publicize their own measures

---

[13] Major steps are usually taken, such as (1) initiating transformation; (2) determining location; (3) developing concepts and synchronizing partners (including activities such as ensuring partner and citizen participation; designing and implementing data governance; preparing funding; developing project concepts; selecting the right technology platform; developing business models; finding partners for implementation; dealing with risks; defining criteria for project selection; performing project selection; developing roadmaps; learning to synchronize); (4) activating resources; (5) realizing projects; and (6) operation and institutionalization (Gassmann et. al. 2019, pp 153–267).

to process and protect personal information. This law (Article 18) also empowers subjects of personal information to request personal information-processing organizations and individuals to update, alter, or cancel their personal information collected or stored by the latter or to stop providing such personal information to a third party. Violators of this law may be given a monetary fine up to 30 million VND (equal to 1,300 USD) for each violation (as stipulated in Articles 84, 85 and 86 of Decree 15/2020/NĐ-CP issued by the Vietnamese Government dated 3 February 2020).

In addition, on 7 March 2019, the Vietnamese government issued Resolution No. 17/NQ-CP regarding certain key tasks and measures of development of the electronic government for the period 2019–2020 with a vision toward 2025. On 8 April 2020, the Vietnamese government issued Decree No. 45/2020/ND-CP on Administrative Procedures by Electronic Means. On 9 April 2020, the Vietnamese Government issued Decree No. 47/2020/ND-CP on Management, Connection, and Share of Digital Data of Regulatory Agencies. The said documents provide legal foundations for operating electronic government and electronic transactions between citizens and governments.

Vietnam has adopted several important laws for cybersecurity, such as the Law on Cyber Information Safety of 2015 and the Law on Cybersecurity of 2018. The current Criminal Code of 2015 (as amended in 2017) has provided for certain legal foundations for handling cyberattacks. Article 285 of this Code provides for a maximum penalty of 7 years of imprisonment applicable to violators involved in "manufacturing, trading, exchanging, giving instruments, equipment, [or] software serving illegal purposes." Article 286 of this code provides for a maximum penalty of 12 years of imprisonment applicable to violators involved in "spreading software programs harmful for computer networks, telecommunications networks or electronic devices." Article 287 of this code provides for a maximum penalty of 12 years of imprisonment applicable to violators who cause "obstruction or disturbance of computer networks, telecommunications networks or electronic devices." Article 288 of this Code provides for a maximum penalty of 7 years of imprisonment applicable to violators involved in "illegal provision or use of information on computer networks or telecommunications networks." Article 289 of this code provides for a maximum penalty of 12 years of imprisonment applicable to violators involved in "illegal infiltration into the computer network, telecommunications network or electronic device of another person." Article 290 of this code provides for a maximum penalty of 20 years of imprisonment applicable to violators involved in "appropriation of property using a computer network, telecommunications network or electronic device." Article 291 of this code provides for a maximum penalty of seven years of imprisonment applicable to violators involved in "illegal collection, possession, exchanging, trading, publishing of information about bank accounts."

Article 80 (11) of Decree 100/2019/ND-CP dated 30 December 2019 on Administrative Penalties for Road Traffic Offences and Rail Transport Offences stipulates that "persons entitled to impose penalties may utilize information and images recorded by sound and image recording devices provided by individuals and organizations to verify and detect the violations specified in this Decree. Minister of public security[14] shall provide procedures for converting results collected from methods and devices other than professional methods and devices handed over by individuals and organizations into evidence to determine administrative violations in road and railway transport." This provision is a legal basis for using images produced by CCTV systems as evidence to prove administrative violations (especially traffic offenses).

The central government has also implemented some steps to support the development of smart cities in Vietnam, especially to enhance the operation of e-government. On 9 December 2019, the National Public Service Portal (https://dichvucong.gov.vn/p/home/dvc-trang-chu.html), an electronic platform to connect the government with people and enterprises, was launched. This portal has certain key components, such as a national database on administrative procedures, one-time login and verification system to connect with ministerial and provincial-level public service portals, an e-payment system, integrated public services of ministries, agencies, and localities, and online supporting services. By August 2020, about 1000 administrative procedures could be handled online. The portal has connected with 18 ministries and agencies, all 60 provinces and centrally run cities, and eight banks and e-wallet service providers (Vietnam News 2020). By 30 December 2020, about 2700 online public services have been provided through the portal. The online payment service had been provided for 14 ministries and 54 out of the 63 provincial-level localities (Vietnam Pictorial 2020). It is expected that basic citizen services (such as birth and death registration and healthcare programs), revenue-earning services (such as property tax and licenses), development services (such as water supply and other utilities and building plan approval), efficiency improvement services (such as procurement and monitoring of projects), back-office improvements (such as accounting and professional management systems) can be fully addressed online in the future. By 30 December 2020, only about 39% of all administrative procedures were provided through the National Public Service Portal.

However, the legal framework for smart city projects in Vietnam is still in an early stage of development. The official criteria to designate an urban area as a "smart city" have not been clarified in any legal normative documents.[15] A system of national standards for the smartness of a city has not been fully developed.[16] There are no special legal normative documents designed for preparing budgets

---

[14] Circular No. 65/2020/TT-BCA dated 19 June 2020.

[15] On 13 September 2019, the Ministry of Information and Communication issued a dispatch (No. 3098/BTTT-KHCN on making public the version 1.0 of Key Performance Indicators [KPI] for smart cities up to 2025). In this dispatch, the Ministry of Information and Communication introduced a definition of a smart urban area (or a smart city) as "an urban area or communities which apply reliable, suitable and innovative ICTs and other methods to increase effectiveness and efficiency of analysis, forecasting and provision of services, management of urban resources with the participation from the people; increase quality of life and working environment for the community; promote innovation for economic development and environmental protection based on interconnection and share of data, information safety and security among systems and services".

[16] On 13 September 2019, the Ministry of Information and Communication issued a dispatch (No. 3098/BTTT-KHCN on making public the version 1.0 of KPI for smart cities up to 2025). However, this dispatch is a kind of reference guide rather than a legal normative document.

for smart city projects. Penalties applicable to violations of protection of personal information are quite lenient. The Decree on Electronic Identity and Verification is still under construction. Another Decree on Personal Data Protection is also still in the drafting stage. The drafting of a Law on Personal Data Protection has not yet been started. There are no legal normative documents for self-driving vehicles. Legal provisions for citizens to participate in decisions made by governments, especially in local governments through electronic means, are still absent in the Law on Local Government of 2015 (as amended in 2019). Smart cities always go hand in hand with an innovative economy, which requires effective systems and good protection of intellectual property. Smart cities also require a safe system of protection of personal data or privacy (especially regulations related to data protection and usage and open data). Smart cities should also be open to new experiments, such as drone usage and autonomous vehicles (Reichental 2020, pp 175–178), for which very few regulations in Vietnam are available.[17]

Perhaps in coming years, governments can conduct a comprehensive evaluation of how much the implementation of smart city projects contribute to solving urban problems in Vietnam, such as overburdened social support systems, transportation congestion, poor public-transport options, inequality, poverty, crime, high cost of healthcare, environmental damage, poor air quality, and aging and broken infrastructure.

There is much room for improvement in the legal framework for smart cities in Vietnam in coming years, especially legal rules for ICT applications (especially digital signatures), urban governance of infrastructure, intellectual property rights, and protection of personal data (data rights law and privacy law).

7.5   Conclusion

The experience of Vietnam shows that promotion of smart city projects requires a huge effort from both the central government and local governments. Some local governments are quite active and interested in experimenting with smart city projects. However, a lack of a sound legal framework could be a hindrance for realizing this ambition. Based on the above analysis, perhaps the central government should play a bigger role in constructing a legal framework that is more favorable to implementation of smart city projects in local governments.

References

Anthopoulos LG (2017) Understanding smart cities: a tool for smart government or an industrial trick? Springer, Switzerland

---

[17] The current Vietnamese legal system does not have any provision for autonomous vehicles.

ASEAN (2018) ASCN ASEAN smart cities framework. https://asean.org/storage/2019/02/ASCN-ASEAN-Smart-Cities-Framework.pdf. Accessed 30 Jan 2021

Communist Party of Vietnam (2021) The dossiers of the national congress of XIII, vol 1. National Political Press, Hanoi

Gassmann O et al (2019) Smart cities: Introducing digital innovation to cities. Bingley, Emerald

General Statistics Office of Vietnam (GSO) (2021) Statistical summary book of Vietnam 2020. Statistical Publishing House, Hanoi

International Organization for Standardization (ISO) (2018) Sustainable cities and communities - Indicators for city services and quality of life. https://www.iso.org/obp/ui/#iso:std:iso:37120:ed-2:v1:en. Accessed 6 Sept 2021

International Telecommunication Union (ITU) (2016) Recommendation ITU-T Y.4900. https://www.itu.int/en/ITU-T/ssc/Pages/info-ssc.aspx. Accessed 6 Sept 2021

Long T (2021) Phat trien do thi thong minh tai Viet Nam (Development of smart cities in Vietnam). http://consosukien.vn/phat-trien-do-thi-thong-minh-tai-viet-nam.htm. Accessed 6 Sept 2021

Reichental J (2020) Smart cities for dummies. John Wiley, Hoboken

ST (2020) Hoi nghi Ban Chi dao xay dung mo hinh thanh pho thong minh tinh Bac Ninh (The conference of Bac Ninh Province's Steering Committee for construction of smart city). http://bacninh.gov.vn/news/-/details/20182/hoi-nghi-ban-chi-ao-xay-dung-mo-hinh-thanh-pho-thong-minh-tinh-bac-ninh. Accessed 6 Sept 2021

Tuan D (2020) Ca nuoc co 862 do thi, dong gop 70% GDP (There are 862 urban areas in Vietnam, producing 70% of GDP). http://baochinhphu.vn/Hoat-dong-cua-lanh-dao-Dang-Nha-nuoc/Ca-nuoc-co-862-do-thi-dong-gop-70-GDP/418045.vgp. Accessed 26 Dec 2020

Vietnam News (2020) 1000th online public service on the National Public Service Portal launched. https://vietnamnews.vn/politics-laws/771333/1000th-online-public-service-on-the-national-public-service-portal-launched.html. Accessed 6 Sept 2021

Vietnam Pictorial (2020) Services on National Public Service Portal now number 2700. https://vietnam.vnanet.vn/english/services-on-national-public-service-portal-now-number-2700/475412.html. Accessed 6 Sept 2021

Chapter 8
Legal Framework for Personal Data Protection in Vietnam

Hoa Chu

Abstract Building a smart city demands the digital transformation of government working processes and procedures, including the digitization and online execution of most administrative procedures. In practice, smart city governance uses information technology to increase the efficacy and efficiency of providing services to the public. The development of smart cities raises concerns among city residents about transparency in data collection and use of personal data. When governments implement smart city projects, sensors and closed-circuit television (CCTV) are placed in most streets, commercial centers, and public areas to observe the behavior of anyone within reach. The public is concerned about what the data collected from these CCTV systems will be used for and how to ensure that such data is not misused, disclosed, leaked, and exploited for the wrong purposes. The issue of protecting personal data and respecting privacy becomes more and more important when personal data is a special type of information. Therefore, Vietnam is urged to take bold actions to effectively strengthen data protection law. This chapter reviews the Vietnamese legal framework for data protection to highlight that the legal framework for data protection in Vietnam should be reformed for the development of smart cities.

8.1 Introduction

The Vietnamese government in recent years has viewed the smart city as an important element of the fourth industrial revolution, utilizing Information and Communications Technology (ICT) and other means to improve the competitiveness, innovation, creativity, transparency, and effectiveness of urban governance as well as to improve efficiency in land use, energy, and resources for the development, improvement, and advancement of the quality of the urban living environment. These many improvements will stimulate socio-economic growth and development. On August 1, 2018, the prime minister issued Decision No. 950/QD-TTg, approving the scheme for the

H. Chu (✉)
Deputy Director General, Institute of Legal Studies, Ministry of Justice, 60 Tran Phu Street, Ba Dinh District, Hanoi, Vietnam
e-mail: chuvihoa@gmail.com

© The Author(s) 2022   91
T. Phan and D. Damian (eds.), *Smart Cities in Asia*, SpringerBriefs in Geography,
https://doi.org/10.1007/978-981-19-1701-1_8

development of smart sustainable cities in Vietnam in the period of 2018 and 2025 with orientations by 2030. This scheme has indicated the goals and roadmap of three phases of smart city development in Vietnam (the period up to 2020; period to 2025; and orientation to 2030). In addition, the project has also shaped seven points of view and principles for smart city development, including the principle "ensure cyber security and data protection."[1]

To turn a traditional city into a smart one requires huge efforts and various tasks. To meet this demand, Vietnam has taken some steps to improve its legal system. However, the legal framework for smart city projects in Vietnam is still at an early stage of development. For example, Decision 950/QD-TTg does not introduce the concept of the smart city, and up to now, Vietnamese law contains no regulation defining the smart city. For that reason, the first of the 10 solutions mentioned in Decision 950/QD-TTg is to review and update the legal system in order to build a legal framework for smart city development in Vietnam. There is room for improvement in the legal framework for smart cities in Vietnam in the following areas: ICT application, urban governance of infrastructure, construction and engineering, and protection of personal data.

In practice, several city or provincial governments in Vietnam have expressed their wishes to transform their provinces or cities into smart cities. To date, 46 out of 63 localities in Vietnam have been planning and implementing smart city projects.[2] These provincial governments have applied information technology in smart city development, including smart city planning, building and managing smart cities, and providing smart city utilities. For example, many localities have completed construction and put into use a Smart City Operation Monitoring Center. The goal of building this center is to supervise and operate smart city services and provide smart city utilities. The Smart City Monitoring Center deploys smart urban services, including five basic smart urban services (citizens' online reporting system, traffic control monitoring, public security monitoring, information monitoring in the network environment, and information security surveillance) and 10 additional smart urban services (environment monitoring and alert system, public service surveillance, smart travel, smart health, smart education, food safety and hygiene, monitoring the spread of COVID-19, open data service, disaster prevention monitoring, and waste truck monitoring system). These smart urban services are aimed at city residents, who benefit from them. However, the same residents who benefit from these services are also raising concerns about their privacy. The Smart City Operation Monitoring Center helps the government supervise and control citizens' social activities and predict

---

[1] See the 4th viewpoint and principle in Section I Article 1 of Decision No. 950/QD-TTg (Prime Minister 2018).

[2] Following are some of the localities that have been implementing smart city projects: Ha Noi, Gia Lai, Thai Binh, Da Nang city, Thanh Hoa, Bac Ninh, Binh Duong, Quang Ninh, Thua Thien Hue, Ho Chi Minh city, Lam Dong, Kien Giang, Lao Cai, Quang Tri, Tien Giang, Vinh Phuc, Yen Bai, Binh Thuan, An Giang, Son La, Hai Duong, Ninh Binh, Ba Ria – Vung Tau, Long An, Nghe An, Bac Giang, Ninh Thuan, Thai Nguyen, Vinh Long, Binh Phuoc, Đong Nai, Đak Nong, Đak Lak, Soc Trang, Cao Bang, Hau Giang, Ha Giang, Ben Tre, Binh Đinh, and Ha Tinh (Ministry of Information and Communications 2021).

social trends. Camera sensors were installed in most streets, commercial centers, and public areas around the province to observe the behavior of anyone within reach for supervising purposes. Urban monitoring through camera sensors is raising concerns among city residents about transparency in data collection and use of personal data.

For example, Da Nang has a traffic monitoring system with 200 cameras embedded with artificial intelligence to automatically detect traffic violations (e.g., driving in the wrong lane, red light violation, speeding, parking vehicles on the sidewalk, parking vehicles in contravention of regulations), to trace vehicles' routes, to count traffic flow, and to automatically control traffic lights. A public security monitoring system with 1,800 cameras and about 34,500 cameras installed on private property has been put into use (Ministry of Information and Communications 2021). Hue city uses 500 cameras with sensors applying face recognition and crowd recognition to supervise the city, ensuring urban security and regulating traffic (Nguyen 2020).

The public is concerned about what the data collected from these cameras will be used for and how to ensure that such data is not misused, disclosed, leaked, and exploited for improper purposes. These public concerns may be based on the following observations. First, agencies, organizations, and enterprises do not have consistent and effective information protection measures. Second, personal data storage and processing systems have vulnerabilities that can be exploited by hackers for their attacks, causing significant losses. Third, personal data theft and illegal trading happens quite frequently. Fourth, personal data is exchanged and utilized in multiple sectors resulting in difficulties in management. Fifth, many organizations collect and use personal data without notification or user protection mechanisms.

If privacy-related concerns are not properly addressed, the smart city implementation risks being opposed and may fail to gather support from city residents. The government of Vietnam is aware that building smart cities requires paying special attention to solving legal problems that might arise from striking a delicate balance between the need to collect and process information and data of citizens and the need to ensure privacy and confidentiality.

At the time of writing, the law on personal data protection still has many loopholes. So far, the legal framework on personal data protection and privacy protection in Vietnam has not been comprehensively developed as it has in some countries around the world. For example, the European Union in 2016 issued a separate Data Protection Regulation—GDPR, effective from May 25, 2018. Thus far, Vietnam has not issued a general law on personal data protection. Relevant regulations regarding personal data protection in Vietnam are scattered in many different legal documents. Therefore, this chapter argues that the legal framework for data protection in Vietnam should be reformed for the development of smart cities.

8.2 Current Status of Vietnamese Laws on Personal Data Protection

A review of nearly 70 Vietnamese legal documents[3] relating to the protection of personal data shows that Vietnamese laws on the protection of personal data are rooted in the right to privacy–a fundamental human right. There is a general principle enshrined in all provisions for personal data protection contained in Vietnam's legal documents: personal data is protected, and other subjects can use personal data as long as the data subject permits them to unless otherwise provided for by law; violators are subject to administrative and criminal penalties, and data subjects suffering from personal data intrusion are entitled to damages.

Constitution 2013 first sets out the general principles that everyone is entitled to the inviolability of personal privacy, personal secrecy, and familial secrecy and has the right to protect his or her honor and prestige. Information regarding personal privacy, personal secrecy, and familial secrecy is safely protected by the law (Article 21 2013). Next, there are four codes, 37 laws, and many sub-law documents addressing and related to personal information.[4] For example, Article 72(1) of the 2006 Law on Information Technology provides that organizations' and individuals' lawful personal information that is exchanged, transmitted, or stored in the network environment shall be kept confidential under law. Article 16 of the 2015 Law on Cyber Information Security provides for the principles of protecting personal information on the internet. Article 19 of the mentioned Law stipulates that personal information-processing organizations and individuals shall take appropriate management and technical measures to protect personal information they have collected and stored and comply with standards and technical regulations on the assurance of cyber information security.

However, the implementation of smart cities creates legal issues for personal data protection, which regulation has so far failed to deal with effectively. First, a question arises in smart cities: does the provision that personal data can only be collected and used with the data subject's consent (or prior consent) still matter in the Internet of Things (IoT) System, particularly when the data is collected in public places (i.e., smart transport systems or smart roads)? If the data subject's consent is not obtained in advance, does the law need to provide general provisions on the collection and use of personal data for public management purposes? What are the responsibilities of individuals and organizations using and protecting personal data in these cases? Currently, Vietnamese law does not have any answers to these questions.

Second, big data, the IoT, the cloud, and the other technological infrastructures in smart cities may endanger the privacy of smart city residents and users, posing a risk to personal data and information. Vietnam is yet to have a law on personal

---

[3] See Appendix.

[4] The Civil Code 2015, The Penal Code 2015 (amended and supplemented in 2017), The Civil Procedure Code 2015, The Criminal Procedure Code 2015, Law on Access to Information 2016, Law on Information Technology 2006, Law on Information Security 2015, Law on Cyber Security 2018, Law on Handling of Administrative Violations 2012, etc.

data protection or a common understanding of "personal data" and "personal data protection." Vietnamese laws currently use about 10 terms, for example "personal information," "private information," "digital information," and "personal information on the internet," with different explanations other than "personal data" (Chu 2021).

For example, "personal information" is used in five legal documents: 2015 Law on Cyber Information Security; Decree No. 85/2016/ND-CP on the Security of information systems by classification; Decree No. 72/2013/ND-CP on the Management, Provision, and use of internet services and online information; Decree No. 52/2013/ND-CP on E-Commerce; and Decree No. 64/2007/ND-CP on information technology application in state agencies' operations. These documents have contradictory explanations of "personal information"; for example, Article 3(13) of Decree No. 52/2013/ND-CP asserts that "personal information referred to in this Decree does not include work contact information and other information that the individual himself/herself has published in the mass media," while Decree No. 72/2013/ND-CP provides that "personal information means information associated with the identification of individuals, including names, ages, addresses, people's identity card numbers, phone numbers, email addresses and other information defined by law," irrespective of whether it has been publicized or not.

Third, current penalties for violations are not deterrent enough. Administrative law and criminal law set out penalties for the intrusion of personal data in the form of human rights or civil rights violations. In Vietnam, non-criminal violations relating to state management are subject to administrative penalties. Administrative penalties concerning personal data protection are scattered throughout many legal documents.[5] The fine could range from VND 2,000,000 to VND 70,000,000 for several personal information intrusion acts, such as retaining users' information for a period exceeding the retention period prescribed by law or agreed upon by two parties; collecting, processing, and using the information of other entities or individuals without obtaining their consent or for illegal purposes; and illegally trading or exchanging private information of users of telecommunications services.

Criminal Code 2015 provides for the "Infringement upon secret information, mail, telephone, telegraph privacy, or other means of private information exchange" in Article 159 and "Illegal provision or use of information on computer networks or telecommunications networks" in Article 288. The maximum penalties are seven years' imprisonment and a fine ranging from VND 20,000,000 to VND 200,000,000. So, the maximum sum of an administrative fine for the intrusion of privacy is VND 70,000,000 (approximately USD 3,000) and that of the criminal fine is VND 200,000,000 (approximately USD 8,600). These fines are quite low compared to

---

[5] See Decree No. 15/2020/ND-CP, on penalties for administrative violations against regulations post and telecommunications, information technology, and radiofrequency; Decree No. 98/2020/ND-CP, prescribing penalties for administrative violations against regulations on production and trade in counterfeit and prohibited goods, and protection of consumer rights; Decree No. 159/2013/ND-CP Providing for administrative penalties for violations arising in the realm of journalism and publishing; Decree No. 158/2013/ND-CP on Penalties for administrative violations about culture, sports, tourism, and advertising; Decree No. 176/2013/ND-CP on Penalties for administrative violations against medical laws, etc.

the fine of EUR 20,000,000 as laid out in GDPR. They do not correspond to the seriousness of the intrusion of privacy or personal data (Chu 2020).

Fourth, there is a lack of provision in law for protection of sensitive personal data, (i.e., personal data concerning racial origins, political views, religious beliefs, social organization participation, or health records). These are likely to be collected by local authorities for e-government systems, e-health, e-welfare, and so on, in smart cities.

Fifth, Vietnam does not have a comprehensive law on personal data protection. Instead, this matter is governed by various laws and decrees (about 70 documents). Nevertheless, all current related provisions are in the form of general—rather than specific—principles. Besides, they are not only insufficient but also contradictory, causing difficulties in law enforcement. For instance, Article 3(17) of the 2015 Law on Cyber Information Security provides that "processing of personal information means the performance of one or some operations of collecting, editing, utilizing, storing, providing, sharing or spreading personal information in cyberspace for commercial purpose." This definition is broader than that in the Articles 21 and 22 of the 2006 Law on Information Technology, which excludes the "collecting" and "utilizing" of personal information. The Law on Information Technology 2006 requires individuals and organizations to notify the personal information subjects of the scope, the purpose, the form, and the place of the collecting and utilizing of personal information before doing so, while the Law on Cyber Information Security 2015 only requires them to have the scope and the purpose notified (Prime Minister's 2020, Working Group 2020, p 24).

Sixth, personal data protection law continues to have some gaps. First and foremost, there are no definitions of "personal data" and "personal data protection." Hence, it is necessary to put forward these definitions and build a common understanding.

- Lack of Penalties for Selling Personal Data

Recently, the selling and buying of personal data have become more common, and the limits of current legal provisions prevent the problem from being dealt with effectively. According to Joint Circular No.10/2012/TTLT-BCA-BQP-BTP-BTT&TT-VKSNDTC-TANDTC on the Application of the Criminal Code provisions on some information technology and telecommunications related crimes, the act of selling and buying personal information does not constitute crimes without proof of it "inflicting serious consequences." For years, the police department for high-tech crime prevention (C50) has made many investigations regarding the selling and buying of personal information on the internet. Due to legal obstacles, those cases often get transferred to departments of information and communications for administrative violation handling (Thi 2018).

- Shortage of Provisions on Criminal Liabilities for the Infringement of Protected Rights to Personal Data

Article 159 of the 2015 Criminal Code provides for the "infringement upon secret information, mail, telephone, telegraph privacy, or other means of private information exchange"; Article 288 designates the "illegal provision or use of information on computer networks or telecommunications networks." However, these two articles have not been updated to include existing illegal acts relating to personal data (Prime Minister's 2020, Working Group 2020, p. 26). For example, Article 159 of the Criminal Code deals with the following acts: appropriation of another person's mails, telegraphs, telex, faxes, or other documents which are transmitted on the postal or telecommunications network in any shape or form; deliberately damaging, losing, or obtaining another person's mails, telegraphs, telex, faxes, or other documents which are transmitted on the postal or telecommunications network; listening or recording conversations against the law; searching, confiscating mails or telegraphs against the law. Article 288 of the Criminal Code deals with the following acts: trading, exchanging, giving, changing, or publishing lawfully private information of an organization or individual on the computer or telecommunications network without the consent of the information owner. In practice, neither of these articles have been updated to include current illegal acts relating to personal data protection, such as stolen social media accounts, personal data theft and illegal trading, and collection and use of personal data without notification or user protection mechanisms.

- Lack of Provisions on Cross-Border Transfer of Personal Data

Practices suggest that private enterprises can participate in supplying public services to smart cities' citizens under Public Private Partnership (PPP) contracts. Who would control the data generated then? How should the cross-border transfers of personal data by enterprises be regulated?

8.3   Recommendations: Making Law on Personal Data Protection

It is urgent to codify the provisions scattered in various legal documents. These provisions themselves are also insufficient. The new law should incorporate the following:

First, the legislation should straightforwardly define the concept of "personal data" and "sensitive personal data" and distinguish between "personal information" and "personal data." Personal data is interpreted to be data on individuals or relating to the identification or ability to identify a specific individual. For example, fundamental personal data should encompass full name, middle name, birth name, alias (if any); date of birth; date of death or missing; blood type, gender; place of birth, birth registration place, habitual residence, temporary residence, hometown, contact address, email address; academic level; nation; nationality; phone number; ID card number, passport number, citizen identification number, driver's license number, license plate number, personal tax code number, social insurance number; marital status; and data that reflects activities or history of activities on cyberspace. In addition, sensitive personal data should include personal data on political and religious opinions; health conditions; genetics; biometrics; gender status; finance; the individual's actual geographical position in the past and present; social relationships; personal data about life, sexual orientation; personal data about crimes, criminal acts, and other personal data as specified by law and in need of necessary security measures.

Second, the new law should improve the provisions on transparency in collecting and utilizing personal data in smart cities. It is necessary to keep the balance between the need to collect and process citizens' information and data to operate a smart city and the need to ensure the right to privacy. To this end, the new law should provide procedures for collecting and sharing personal data.

Third, it is necessary to improve the provisions on (1) rights and obligations of parties concerning personal data, including rights of data subjects; obligations of the government and subjects collecting and processing data; obligations of third parties; and (2) acts prohibited. Vietnamese law recognizes the general principle of prohibiting the providing, trading, transferring, storing, using of information that violates the provisions on information safety and security. Nonetheless, all current legal documents center on the protection of national and military secrets. The new law should specifically provide for acts prohibited in collecting and processing personal data to create a legal base for setting out penalties (Chu 2020).

Appendix of Documents Reviewed

1. Circular No. 10/2016/TT-BGDDT dated April 5, 2016, issuing Regulations for student affairs in formal higher education programs.
2. Circular No. 35/2016/TT-NHNN dated December 29, 2016, on safety and confidentiality over the provision of banking services on the Internet.
3. Circular No. 57/2015/TT-BYT dated December 30th, 2015, detailing Decree No. 10/2015/ND-CP for childbirth by in vitro fertilization and conditions for surrogacy for humanitarian reasons.
4. Constitution dated November 28, 2013, of the Socialist Republic of Vietnam.
5. Decision No. 58/2007/QD-BGTVT of November 21, 2007, promulgating the regulation on inspection of quality, technical safety, and environmental protection in manufacture and assembly of motorcycles and mopeds.
6. Decree No. 10/2015/ND-CP dated January 28, 2015, on giving birth through in vitro fertilization and conditions for altruistic gestational surrogacy.
7. Decree No. 111/2010/ND-CP of November 23, 2010, detailing and guiding several articles of the law on judicial records.
8. Decree No. 123/2015/ND-CP dated November 15, 2015, on guidelines for law on civil status.

9. Decree No. 137/2015/ND-CP detailing several articles of, and providing measures for implementing, the Law on Citizen Identification.
10. Decree No. 158/2013/NĐ-CP of November 12, 2013, on penalties for administrative violations about culture, sports, tourism, and advertising.
11. Decree No. 159/2013/ND-CP dated November 12, 2013, providing for administrative penalties for violations arising in the realm of journalism and publishing.
12. Decree No. 176/2013/ND-CP dated November 14, 2013, penalties for administrative violations against medical laws.
13. Decree No. 20/2012/ND-CP dated March 20, 2012, prescribing the database on the execution of criminal judgments.
14. Decree No. 23/2015/ND-CP dated February 16, 2015, issuing copies from master registers, certification of true copies from originals, authentication of signatures, and contracts.
15. Decree No. 52/2013/ND-CP of May 16, 2013, on e-commerce.
16. Decree No. 56/2008/ND-CP of April 29, 2008, stipulating the organization and operation of tissue banks and the national coordination center for human organ transplantation.
17. Decree No. 64/2007/ND-CP of April 10, 2007, on information technology application in state agencies' operations.
18. Decree No. 72/2013/NĐ-CP of July 15, 2013, on the management, provision, and use of internet services and online information.
19. Decree No. 76/2012/ND-CP of October 03, 2012, detailing the implementation of several articles of the law on denunciations.
20. Decree No. 85/2016/ND-CP dated July 01, 2016, on the security of information systems by classification.
21. Decree No. 98/2020/ND-CP of August 26, 2020, prescribing penalties for administrative violations against regulations on production and trade in counterfeit and prohibited goods, and protection of consumer rights.
22. Decree No.15/2020/ND-CP of February 03, 2020, on Penalties for administrative violations against regulations post and telecommunications, information technology, and radiofrequency.
23. Decree of Government No. 35/2007/ND-CP of March 08, 2007, on banking e-transactions.
24. Joint Circular No. 06/2008/TTLT-BTTTT-BCA of November 28, 2008, on the assurance of infrastructure safety and information security in the post, telecommunications, and information technology activities.
25. Law No. 03/2007/QH12 of November 21, 2007, on prevention and control of infectious diseases.
26. Law No. 06/2012/QH13 of June 18, 2012, on Deposit Insurance.
27. Law No. 07/2012/QH13 of June 18, 2012, on Prevention of Money Laundering
28. Law No. 08/2012/QH13 of June 18, 2012, on Higher Education.
29. Law No. 100/2015/QH13 dated November 27, 2015, Criminal Code (amended in 2017).
30. Law No. 101/2015/QH13 dated 27 November 2015, Criminal Procedure Code.

31.   Law No. 102/2016/QH13 dated April 05th, 2016, Children Law.
32.   Law No. 103/2016/QH13 dated April 05th, 2016, Press Law.
33.   Law No. 104/2016/QH13 dated April 06th, 2016, on Access to Information.
34.   Law No. 105/2016/QH13 dated April 06th, 2016, on Pharmacy.
35.   Law No. 13/2012/QH13 of July 20, 2012, on Judicial Expertise (amended in 2020).
36.   Law No. 19/2012/QH13 of November 20, 2012, on Publishing.
37.   Law No. 21-LCT/HDNN8 of June 30, 1989, of people's health.
38.   Law No. 25/2018/QH14 dated June 12, 2018, on Denunciation.
39.   Law No. 28/2009/QH12 of June 17, 2009, on judicial records.
40.   Law No. 38/2005/QH11 of June 14, 2005, on Education, amended in 2009.
41.   Law No. 38/2019/QH14 dated June 13, 2019, on Tax administration.
42.   Law No. 40/2009/QH12 of November 23, 2009, on medical examination and treatment.
43.   Law No. 41/2009/QH12 of November 23, 2009, on telecommunications.
44.   Law No. 47/2010/QH12 of June 16, 2010, on credit institutions; Law No. 17/2017/QH14 dated November 20, 2017 amendments to some articles of the Law on credit institutions.
45.   Law No. 49/2010/QH12 of June 17, 2010, on Post.
46.   Law No. 50/2005/QH11 of November 29, 2005, on Intellectual property.
47.   Law no. 51/2005/QH11 of November 29, 2005, on E-transactions.
48.   Law No. 54/2014/QH13 dated June 23, 2014, on Customs.
49.   Law No. 54/2019/QH14 dated November 26, 2019, on Securities.
50.   Law No. 58/2014/QH13 dated November 20, 2014, on Social Insurance.
51.   Law No. 59/2014/QH13 dated November 20, 2014, on Citizen identification.
52.   Law No. 64/2006/QH11 of June 29, 2006, on HIV/AIDS prevention and control.
53.   Law No. 67/2006/QH11 of June 29, 2006, on information technology.
54.   Law No. 67/2011/QH12 of March 29, 2011, on Independent Audit.
55.   Law No. 75/2006/QH11 of November 29, 2006, on a donation, removal, and Transplantation of human tissues and organs and donation and recovery of cadavers.
56.   Law No. 81/2006/QH11 of November 29, 2006, on the residence.
57.   Law No. 81/2015/QH13 dated June 24, 2015, on State Audit Office of Vietnam.
58.   Law No. 86/2015/QH13 dated November 19, 2015, on Cyber Information Security.
59.   Law No. 89/2015/QH13 dated November 23, 2015, on Statistics.
60.   Law No. 91/2015/QH13 dated November 24, 2015, Civil Code.
61.   Law No. 92/2015/QH13 dated November 25th, 2015, Civil Procedure Code.
62.   Law No. 93/2015/QH13 dated November 25, 2015, on Administrative Procedures.
63.   Law No.24/2000/QH10 of December 09, 2000, on Insurance Business (amended in 2010, 2019).
64.   Law No.59/2010/QH12 of November 17, 2010, on Protection of Consumers' Rights.

65. Ordinance No.04/2002/PL-UBTVQH11 of November 04, 2002, on the organization of The Military Courts.

References

Article 21 (2013) The constitution of the socialist republic of Vietnam. https://constitutionnet.org/sites/default/files/tranlation_of_vietnams_new_constitution_enuk_2.pdf

Chu HT (2020) Report on legal framework for personal data protection in VietNam. Paper presented at the workshop on Sharing best practices in personal data protection on cyberspace, with focus on disadvantaged and vulnerable groups in VietNam, Hanoi, 09 December 2020.

Chu HT (2021) What solution to handle the situation of buying and selling personal information?. http://baochinhphu.vn/Phap-luat/Giai-phap-nao-xu-ly-tinh-trang-mua-ban-du-lieu-thong-tin-ca-nhan/433995.vgp

Ministry of Information and Communications (2021) Report on the state of smart city implementation in Vietnam

Nguyen AD (2020) Personal data protection in smart city—Experience and recommendations from Thua Thien Hue's case. Paper presented at the workshop on personal data protection and privacy in digital transformation and development of the digital economy: discussion and policy recommendations, Hanoi, 15 July 2020.

Prime Minister (2018) Decision No. 950/QD-TTg approving the project for sustainable smart urban development in Vietnam from 2018 through 2025, with a vision to 2030

Prime Minister's 2020 Working Group (2020) Report on legal regulation review in preparing for the Fourth Industrial Revolution

Thi C (2018) The situation of buying and selling personal information is rampant. https://kiemsat.vn/tran-lan-tinh-trang-mua-ban-thong-tin-ca-nhan-50866.html

Chapter 9
Digital Transformation in Banking: A Case from Vietnam

Minh Son Ha and Thuy Linh Nguyen

Abstract This article aims to examine the literature on digital transformation in the banking sectors and the current commercial banks' digital transformation landscape in Vietnam. The paper provides examples of some local commercial banks to show that digital banking should be considered an integral part of smart cities. The paper also analyzes the challenges facing Vietnamese banks in their digitalization process to become smarter banks. Next, the study makes some recommendations about how to leverage the digitalization process in the Vietnamese banking system. It can be concluded from this research that digital transformation is key to the banking industry creating value for the customer and keeping pace with innovation in smart cities where people expect real-time, instant gratification. This paper also suggests further research directions.

9.1 Introduction

In today's world, the new metric for developed economies is no longer Gross Domestic Product (GDP) or economic growth, but the ability to enable automation, invest in smart infrastructure, capitalize transformation, and leverage new technologies to become smart economies. Banks with their financial services are a key part of the infrastructure of smart economies. To perform significant roles in smart economies, they have to address their digitalization process as a matter of urgency if they are not to be left behind in a market that finds itself in the full throes of transformation. In Vietnam, the digital transformation of the banking system is expected to change the management of banks to be leaner and smarter to fit into a world where technology is pervasive and ubiquitous as well as to support the ambition of smart cities.

M. S. Ha
Department Deputy, Academy of Finance, Hanoi, Vietnam
e-mail: haminhson@hvtc.edu.vn

T. L. Nguyen (✉)
Academy of Finance, Hanoi, Vietnam
e-mail: nguyenthuylinhnhbh@hvtc.edu.vn

© The Author(s) 2022
T. Phan and D. Damian (eds.), *Smart Cities in Asia*, SpringerBriefs in Geography,
https://doi.org/10.1007/978-981-19-1701-1_9

A strong wave of digital transformation in the Vietnamese banking system has taken place in the last three years. Most Vietnamese banks have either implemented or are in the process of developing their digital transformation strategies. There are three basic approaches to the digital transformation of banking in Vietnam. The first involves the digitalization of front-end channel developments. The second approach is focusing on digital transformation in the internal process. The third approach is a combination of the first and the second along with the development of stand-alone, digital-only banks. Given the analytic framework of the banking digitalization process in Vietnam, a case study of some Vietnamese commercial banks indicates that banks must transform to provide embedded banking utility driven by behavior, location, sensors, machine learning, and artificial intelligence (AI). This transformation is essential for smart cities to thrive and develop.

After reviewing the current landscape, the article considers the challenges of Vietnamese banks in their digitalization. The foremost challenge is legal framework—a major barrier to accelerating digital transformation in Vietnam. Network security is also an obstacle for the process of digitalization in banking, due to increasing operational fraud, customer fraud, cyberattacks on banking infrastructure, and leaked user data. In addition, Industrial Revolution 4.0 and the Fintech trend promote strong competition for banks. Fintech companies are posing challenges for the banking community by attracting customers and expanding market share, especially in online lending transactions and peer-to-peer lending. The study makes some recommendations to overcome the challenges and leverage the digitalization process in the Vietnamese banking system. It can be concluded from this research that digital transformation is the key for the banking industry to create value for the customer, keep pace with innovation, and perform their role in promoting the development of smart cities.

9.2 Digital Transformation in Banking Concepts

Digital transformation changes the whole business landscape of any organization, regardless of industry, size, maturity, or market. Researchers and practitioners interpret the concept of digital transformation in different ways. While Westerman et al. refer to digital transformation as the "use of technology in order to radically improve performance or reach of enterprises" (2011, p 12), experts at Pricewaterhouse Coopers contend that this process "establishes new technologies based on the Internet with a fundamental impact on the society as a whole" (2013, p 25). Westerman et al. also believe that digital transformation is an "on going digital evolution both strategically and tactically" (2011, p 23).

To maintain the banking industry's competitiveness, traditional banks should become more agile, embrace innovative culture, and focus on the simplification of providing services anytime in any place to potential clients (Mirković and Lukić

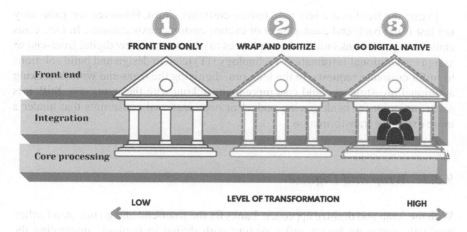

Fig. 9.1 The three levels of digital transformation. *Source* Illustrated by the author

2015). To achieve all those goals, banks found new support in modern big data[1] technologies. For many organizations, especially banks, big data and data analytics technologies represent a new source of competitive advantage. Digital banking transformation involves the integration of data, advanced analytics, and digital technology into all areas of a financial institution, changing the way work is done, priorities are set, and services are delivered (Australian Government 2020).

Experts at Pricewaterhouse Coopers contend that "digital transformation is used to influence three organisational dimensions" (2013, p 36). The first or external dimension, means "focusing on customer experience digitally." The second or internal dimension means "the organisational processes and structures." The third or global dimension, means "all sectors and functions." In general, digital transformation leads to superior performance by influencing organizational dimensions "internally, externally, and comprehensively." In banks, there are three levels of digital transformation, namely front-end only, wrap and digitize, and go digital native as shown in Fig. 9.1 (Pham Tien Dung 2020).

9.2.1 Digitize Front-End Only

The simplest approach of digital transformation is the front-end only, focusing on the primary ways a customer interacts with a bank, such as website and app. Mostly a cosmetic fix, digitizing the front-end only means the bank designs an appealing mobile app and web interface but keeps the organization's workflows, culture, and back-end infrastructure intact.

---

[1] Big data refers to massive complex structured and unstructured data sets that are rapidly generated and transmitted from a wide variety of sources.

Fixing the front-end might help reduce customer churn. However, the gains may not last if the back-end cannot meet or exceed customer expectations. In fact, costs could increase if banks must add employees to maintain the new digital front-end or assign an additional Information Technology (IT) team to design and build solutions to fulfill customer requests. In the long run, digitizing the front-end without making additional investments could cost more than sticking with the status quo. Still, it is a starting point for banks facing budget or organizational constraints that hinder a more extensive transformation.

9.2.2 Wrap and Digitize

With the wrap and digitize approach, banks fix the front-end and go one step further, gradually replacing legacy infrastructure with digital technology, integrating the middle and back offices along the way. In this approach, employees might be transitioned to higher-value roles in new centers of excellence, as this conversion eliminates the need for certain manual tasks. As wrap and digitize focuses on individual improvements, it can take some time before the full scope of the bank's processes has been overhauled.

9.2.3 Go Digital Native

In this approach, financial institutions build digital native banks that fully utilize digital customer interfaces and back-end. This strategy can deliver significant cost savings as well as the ability for the bank to adapt quickly when change comes.

Reducing costs is one reason to go digital native, but the main reason is enhancing agility. Digital native lets banks adapt to rapidly changing customer tastes, and furthermore, it allows them to test and iterate. The digital core and open architecture also allow flexible approaches for partnering with third parties to offer a range of products and services. It is possible to set up a fully functional, digital native bank using third-party architecture in the cloud.

Over the last 50 years, with the development of technology, the banking system has witnessed significant changes. We have moved from the branch as the only channel available for access to banking services to multi-channel[2] and then omni-channel[3] capability, corresponding to the different levels of digitalization. At the first level,

---

[2] Multi-channel means that a bank provides services to its customers through more than one channel, which typically include branches, automated teller machines (ATMs), call centers, internet banking and—increasingly—mobile.

[3] Omni-channel banking is built on a multichannel strategy that allows anytime, anywhere, any device access with consistent experience across channels. Omni-channel enables interactions across multiple customer touch points where intents are captured, insights are derived, and conversations are personalized and optimized.

banks are simply adding technology on top of the old traditional banking model, and the final level takes banks to digital omni-channel for customers exclusively accessing banking via digital. Understanding these three levels allows us to figure out the road map for Vietnamese banks to retrofit into smart cities. It is obvious that, like every other service platform, banking is being placed in smart economies that expect real-time, instant gratification.

9.3 The Current Commercial Banks' Digital Transformation Landscape in Vietnam

In the last five years in Vietnam, branch-based expansion is no longer a target strategy of banks, and there has been a considerable need to facilitate access to the core utility of the bank. This need, combined with the design possibilities afforded by technologies like mobile, allowed for some spectacular rethinking of how banking could be better embedded in smart cities. The current landscape in banking digital transformation gives us a concise overview of the positions of Vietnamese banks in the process of technological adaption.

Vietnam's banking sector consists of four state-owned commercial banks, 31 joint-stock commercial banks, nine wholly-foreign-owned banks, two joint-venture banks, two policy banks and one cooperative bank. In addition, there are 48 foreign bank branches currently operating in Vietnam (see Fig. 9.2).

Vietnam has many favorable conditions for the development of digital banking, thanks to its population of 96 million people with a golden population structure (56 million people participating in the labor market) (General Statistics Office of Vietnam 2020). According to the report of the payment department of the State Bank of Vietnam (SBV), in 2019, Vietnam's online population reached a total of 64 million

Fig. 9.2 Vietnamese banks by assets 2019. *Source* State Bank of Vietnam (2020)

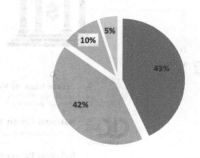

Vietnamese bank by assets 2019

- State - owned commercial banks
- Joint-stock commerical banks
- Wholly - foreign - owned banks
- Others

internet users. E-commerce sales have a high growth rate of 30% a year. Seventy two percent of the Vietnamese population owns a smartphone but most Vietnamese—69% of the adult population—do not have a bank account. At the same time, Vietnam has a technical foundation for digital banking development with almost 19,000 ATMs and 270,000 point-of-sale (POS) terminals in place in 2019. To date, 78 banks offer internet payment solutions. Mobile payment is available at 47 banks, and 29 banks accept quick response (QR) code payment with 30,000 QR code payments in 2019 (see Fig. 9.3).

Real-time payment systems are enabled by the National Payment Corporation of Vietnam (NAPAS) while the National Credit Information Center of Vietnam (CIC) provides credit information infrastructure. The country's national identification database is still under development.

In Vietnam, a strong wave of digital transformation has taken place within banks in the last three years. The majority of Vietnamese banks have either implemented or are in the process of developing their digital transformation strategies. In fact, by the end of 2019,

- 40.6% of Vietnamese credit institutions have approved the digital transformation strategy;
- 31.9% have implemented the digital transformation strategy;
- 20.3% are planning to develop a digital strategy;
- and only 7.2% of the credit institutions have not taken into account building the digital strategy (see Fig. 9.4).

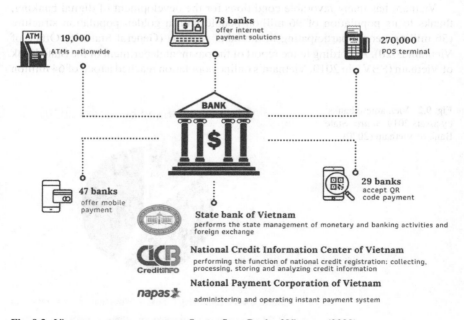

Fig. 9.3 Vietnamese payment system. *Source* State Bank of Vietnam (2020)

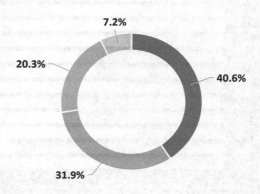

Process of research and implementation of the digital transformation strategy

7.2%

20.3%

40.6%

31.9%

- Credit institutions that have approved the digital transformation strategy,
- Credit institutions that have implemented digital transformation strategies
- Credit institutions that are planning to develop a digital strategy
- Credit institutions that have not taken into account building the digital strategy

Fig. 9.4 Process of research and implementation of the digital research strategy. *Source* State Bank of Vietnam (2020)

With the planning of digital strategies, Vietnamese commercial banks expect to reap the benefits of digital transformation in the next three to five years. While 82.5% of banks expect revenue growth of at least 10%, 58.1% of banks expect that over 60% of customers will use digital channels, and 44.4% of banks expect the customer growth rate to be more than 50%.[4]

Currently, about 70% of credit institutions have average willingness to deploy technologies such as Open API, Data Analytics, ISO 20022, and Mobility (see Fig. 9.5).

Pham Tien Dung (2020) pointed out that there are three basic approaches to the digital transformation of banking in Vietnam.[13] The first involves the digitalization of front-end channel developments and includes innovation in mobile banking, e-know your customer (eKYC), QR code payment, virtual assistants/chatbots, and 24/7 call centers[5] (front-end only).

The second approach focuses on digital transformation in the internal process with developments including online real-time trading systems, robotic process automation, and the application of artificial intelligence and third-party data in risk management (wrap and digitize). Digitizing the information database and the utilization

---

[4] Data was summarized from the workshop proceedings of the national conference (2021), Transforming the banking industry in uncertainty: turning risks into opportunities.

[5] Data was summarized from workshop proceedings of the national conference (2020), Digital transformation of the banking industry in the context of uncertainty.

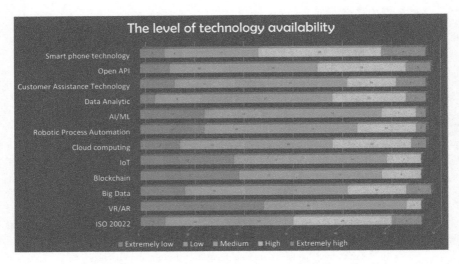

Fig. 9.5 The level of technology availability. *Source* State Bank of Vietnam (2020)

of technologies and tools such as big data warehousing, automated data collection, cloud computing, data analytics, artificial intelligence, open application programming interface (API) and blockchain are still in their infancy. However, looking forward, they present significant growth potential.

The third approach is a combination of the first and the second along with the development of stand-alone, digital-only banks (go digital native). TPBank and Vietinbank are examples of the first approach while Vietcombank and Techcombank are examples of the second approach. TPBank and Vietinbank operate on an omni-channel platform to ensure a consistent customer experience. They aim to become smarter at analyzing customer behavior and obtaining customer insights. This will enable them to provide personalized products and services and, in turn, gain a competitive advantage in the market (Australian Government 2020).

VPBank, with the launch of the digital-only bank Timo (Timo is now cooperating with Bản Việt Bank), as well as the recently launched YOLO are two examples of the third approach.

Notable Initiatives of Digital Transformation in Banking in Vietnam

LiveBank: TPBank

TPBank launched LiveBank in 2017. The bank provides 24/7 automated banking services through approximately 250 LiveBank stations nationwide. LiveBank offers the usual functions of an ATM. Additionally, customers can open new deposit accounts, scan thumbprints, and obtain new debit cards on the spot. LiveBank applies innovative technologies such as eKYC, optical character recognition (OCR), QR code, cash recycler, and biometrics.

iPay: A Mobile Banking App from Vietinbank

Vietinbank launched the latest version of its iPay mobile banking app in December 2019. The bank added 50 new functionalities and improved the user experience through consumer deals, high speed, and strong security.

Timo: A Fully Digital Bank

Through the strategic partnership with VP Bank, Timo was launched in 2016 as Vietnam's first digital lifestyle bank. This service includes a mobile app and allows customers to request a new debit card. Two of Timo's unique functions are its versatile online account management and "Timo Hangouts," which are described as laid-back "atmosphere spaces" instead of traditional bank branches. New customers can make an appointment to attend a "Timo Hangout" to complete KYC requirements.

BIDV: Digital Banking Centre

BIDV established its Digital Banking Centre in 2019 as an innovation hub to build advanced and modern customer-centric products. BIDV launched the "BIDV Home" mobile app, allowing customers to get a home loan easily with mobile devices. Using BIDV Home, customers can apply for BIDV-financed housing loans at competitive interest rates, get consultation online before visiting a transaction office, and track the loan application progress.

9.4 Challenges in Banking Digital Transformation

The current banking transformation landscape demonstrates that Vietnamese banking systems are adapting to the smart world by removing friction and enabling utility to offer better margins, better customer satisfaction, and more dynamic scaling potential. However, the data also reveals that most Vietnamese banks are at the first and second level of digital transformation. To reach the highest level, native digital, banks face major challenges.

9.4.1 Legal Framework

The incomplete legal framework is a major barrier to digital banking transformation in Vietnam. There has been a widening gap between the velocity of financial markets and regulatory change. Although the Vietnamese government and its regulators support and encourage industry adoption of advanced technologies, the regulators have elaborated on rigid regulatory systems built in an analog era where everything was paper-based. This system has worked well in the past, but some features make them ill-suited to today's challenges. We need to create digitally-native regulation to regulate digital markets and to deploy new technology in the regulatory process.

In March 2017, the SBV established the Fintech Steering Committee. The committee was set up to study and improve the fintech ecosystem and to create an enabling framework to support digital transformation in banking and fintech development in Vietnam. In August 2018, the prime minister of Vietnam issued Decision 986/QD-TTg approving the "development strategy for the Vietnam banking industry to 2025 with the vision toward 2030" (the Banking Strategy). In January 2019, Decision 34/QD-NHNN was published. This decision outlined an action plan to implement the Banking Strategy.

The government of Vietnam has also introduced broader reforms to support the growth of digital banking and financial services. In December 2018, for example, SBV issued Decision 2617/QĐ-NHNN on the "action plan of the banking industry to realize Directive 16/CT-TTG of the government on enhancing the nation's capability to embrace the 4th industrial revolution technologies by 2020 with the vision towards 2025."

Although these efforts to retrofit the regulatory system have gained notable successes, Vietnamese financial regulatory frameworks are still risk-adverse, deliberate, and clear. While the government has mandates to promote goals like competition and financial inclusion, the SBV still has as its primary mission to detect and address risk to the financial system and its customers. They are not meant to spot new digital products and services that deserve a regulatory amendment. Despite the development of autonomous networks, smart contracts, smart assets, and infrastructure in finance areas, Vietnam has not yet completed the legal framework for banks to share, store, and exploit data with services such as banking, telecommunications, and insurance. Vietnam is challenged to respond to the accelerated digital transformation by creating clear legal frameworks for user data and information security.

In the future, further regulations should be introduced to improve IT and payment infrastructure and optimize ATM and POS networks. Law should be adopted to tighten information protection and cyber security. It is also important to institute regulatory frameworks to foster the development of digital banking and the fintech ecosystem associated with comprehensive financial inclusion.

9.4.2   Network Security

In Vietnam, along with the rise of smart cities, there is greater need for cybersecurity as more businesses and consumers engage in the digital economy, and as critical systems such as finance and government are increasingly digitalized. In the 2017 Global Cybersecurity Index, Vietnam ranked 101 out of 193 nations (International Telecommunication Union 2017). As well, in 2016 the proportion of computers affected by dangerous viruses in Vietnam was 63.2%, three times the global average.

According to the BKAV Corporation—an IT company and network security expert— the cost of cyberattacks in Vietnam increased by 15% to US$540 million between 2016 and 2017 (BKAV 2017).

In banking, security risks such as fraud, customer fraud, cyberattacks on banking infrastructure and leaked user data are increasing. According to Ernst and Young (2018), 8319 cyberattacks occurred on banks last year and 560,000 computers were affected by malware capable of stealing bank account information. Banks faced losses of US$642 million caused by computer viruses, while only 52% of customers worried about security while using online banking.

The banking digitalization process along with the evolution of the payment space means regulators will have to deal with increasingly diverse types of value stores and payment vehicles, many of them exposed to security risks. What we need at a minimum is country-wide AI-based monitoring to keep criminals and terrorists out of the financial system.

Another solution for increasing network security is cybersecurity education, which is quite new in Asian countries including Vietnam and has not been adequately focused. A 2015 survey by ESET indicated that 78% of internet users in Asia do not have any formal cybersecurity education (ESET 2015). Low capability makes the region vulnerable to cyberattacks, especially Vietnam. Cybersecurity training programs should be organized frequently in cybersecurity training centers. Antivirus software for homes, businesses, and smartphones and public digital signature verification services should be developed by IT companies such as BKAV Corporation and CMC.

9.4.3 The Participation of Fintech and Bigtech Companies

Industrial revolution 4.0 and the Fintech trend promote strong competition. Fintech companies are posing great challenges for the banking community by attracting customers and expanding market share, especially in online lending transactions and peer-to-peer lending, areas that were formerly considered traditional businesses handled in the past by commercial banks. Therefore, if commercial banks do not continue to proactively apply new technology, invest in modern equipment, and set up cooperation with Fintech companies, they will be left behind in the technology competition.

9.5 Conclusions

Increased use of computers, machine learning, robots, and artificial intelligence in all spheres and aspects has significantly changed modern banking business in smart cities. The growth of banks will unblock bottlenecks to promote the development of smart cities. Banks and governments should react promptly to create new opportunities in the process of banking digitalization. To leverage the banking digitalization process, it is also important to carry out a makeover of the technology platform by converting it to a more modular and flexible infrastructure that enables the integration of new technologies and speedy development of new products.

References

Australian Government, Austrade (2020) Digital banking in Vietnam, a guide to market

BKAV (2017) Viet Nam cyber security overview in 2017 and predictions for 2018, BKAV Global Task Force Blog

Ernst and Young (2018) ASEAN fintech census 2018

ESET (2015) ESET Asia cyber-savviness report 2015, ESET: Bratislava, Slovakia

General Statistics Office of Vietnam (2020) Labor and employment survey report 2020

International Telecommunication Union (2017) Global cybersecurity index (GCI) 2017

Mirković V, Lukić J (2015) Key characteristics of organizational structure that supports digital transformation. Ekonomski vidici XX(2–3)

Pham Tien Dung (2020) Digital banking in Vietnam, conference proceedings digital transformation of the banking industry in the context of uncertainty: turning risks into opportunities

Pricewaterhousecoopers (2013) Annual Report 2013

State Bank of Vietnam (2020) Digitalization in Vietnam payment department

Westerman G et al (2011) Digital transformation: a roadmap for billion-dollar organization. MITSloan Manage Rev

Chapter 10
Developing Smart City Infrastructure Inside a Historical City: A Case from Thua Thien Hue, Vietnam

Nguyen Thi Bich Ngoc

Abstract With the accelerated development of science and technology in the last 20 years, many cities in the world are undergoing major changes to become smarter, safer, and more sustainable. Some cities in Vietnam are also making efforts to catch up with this irreversible trend. In Vietnam, the government is working with corporations to plan and implement smart cities, focusing on nine fields: architecture, urban planning, interaction, healthcare, education, transportation, safety and security, journalism and communication management, and digital government. This paper draws on the case of the Intelligent Operations Center in Thua Thien Hue province—a remarkable example of effective smart city planning and application in Asia—and analyzes its smart city implementation inside a historical and cultural city. The center is designed and implemented to lay a sound foundation for smart city technologies. The Intelligent Operations Center helps the government supervise and control citizens' social activities and predict social trends. Additionally, it encourages the participation of citizens in managing the city.

10.1 Introduction

Thua Thien Hue is a cultural and historical center of Vietnam, which has five world heritage sites. The province is committed to sustainable tourism development. An assessment of Thua Thien Hue province sheds light on how the city authorities can develop intangible smart city infrastructure while preserving cultural and historical values so citizens live in a comfortable and sustainable environment while tourists enjoy a better cultural travel experience. This article analyzes Thua Thien Hue's transformation in e-government. First, it describes smart city development in Vietnam. Then, the case study analysis is presented in detail, describing the Intelligent Operations Center's (IOC) solutions to six main problems. The major features of the IOC are using cameras with sensors applying face recognition and crowd recognition to supervise the city, ensure urban security, and regulate traffic; managing journalism

N. T. B. Ngoc (✉)
Academy of Policy and Development, Hanoi, Vietnam
e-mail: ngocntb@apd.edu.vn

T. Phan and D. Damian (eds.), *Smart Cities in Asia*, SpringerBriefs in Geography,
https://doi.org/10.1007/978-981-19-1701-1_10

and media; supervising public administration services, information technology (IT) security issues control, and governance; using smartphone applications to develop stronger bonds with residents and tourists; and installing environmental sensors for early natural disaster preparation, real-time analyzing, and warning. Last, the article gives some recommendations for the authority to better engage residents and tourists in co-creating the province. The results of the case study indicate that Thua Thien Hue has been effectively implementing the smart city strategy with an aim to preserve cultural and historical values of local areas.

10.2 Smart City Development in Vietnam

The idea of the smart city has been conceptualized by prestigious scholars and organizations, but there is still no unified definition. One author defines it as follows:

[A] smart city is a well-defined geographical area, in which high technologies such as [information and communication technologies] ICT, logistic, energy production, and so on, cooperate to create benefits for citizens in terms of well-being, inclusion and participation, environmental quality, intelligent development; it is governed by a well-defined pool of subjects, able to state the rules and policy for the city government and development. (Dameri 2013, p 2549)

The European Commission defines a smart city as "a place where traditional networks and services are made more efficient with the use of digital and telecommunication technologies for the benefit of its inhabitants and business" (European Commission nd, para 1). A smart city is not limited to employing ICT for better resource use and fewer emissions. It also means more intelligent urban transportation, better water supply and waste disposal facilities, and more efficient lighting and heating in buildings. Besides, it means a more interactive and responsive city administration with the participation of inhabitants, which creates safer public places and satisfies the needs of an aging population.

According to the International Telecommunication Union (ITU), a smart sustainable city can be seen as "an innovative city that uses information and communication technologies (ICTs) and other means to improve quality of life, efficiency of urban operation and services, and competitiveness, while ensuring that it meets the needs of present and future generations with respect to economic, social, environmental as well as cultural aspects" (ITU-T nd, para 1).

Most definitions of smart city emphasize the close relationship between governance and technology in improving citizens' well-being and sustainable development. The first and second definitions highlight the importance of the inhabitants' participation in developing smart cities. If the authority is considered the smart city service provider, the city inhabitants are customers when developing smart city models.

Customer participation is "the degree to which the customer is involved in producing and delivering the service" (Dong et al. 2008, p 160). In other words, it includes all kinds of customer involvement and engagement in the value-creation process, including four main dimensions: information seeking, information sharing, responsible behavior, and personal interaction. Through information seeking, co-creators actively get information about how and what to do during the co-creation process to reach the desired performance. Information sharing involves customers providing essential information to service firms or employees (Yi et al. 2011) who use the information to create new ideas or perform their duties (Ragatz et al. 2002). Customers show responsible behavior when they recognize their duties and requirements and behave cooperatively, in line with existing rules and policies and according to the directions offered by employees (Bettencourt 1997; Ennew and Binks 1999). Finally, personal interaction refers to interpersonal relations between customers and employees; it is a cornerstone of successful value co-creation (Ennew and Binks 1999; Hsieh et al. 2018).

With the accelerated development of science and technology in the last 20 years, many cities in the world are undergoing major changes to become smarter, safer, and more sustainable (nexusintegra nd). Some cities in Vietnam are also making efforts to catch up with this irreversible trend. Economic development is the main driver of infrastructure development in Vietnam, including smart city infrastructure. The global competition organization IDM has pointed out that the smart city ranking index will be one of the decisive indicators in attracting investment capital and high-quality human resources. This index will become the core standard for countries to compete in the industrial age 4.0. Economic and technology experts assess that Vietnam is highly motivated to focus on developing smart cities in the future (Journal of Building Materials 2020).

Recently, Vietnam has been very active in developing smart cities. According to data collected by Viettel Group, a favorable factor for smart city development in Vietnam is the large percentage of internet users/total population in Vietnam (Top 10 in Asia). Vietnam currently has about 49 million internet users with a penetration density of 51.5% (Nguyen 2019). The government of Vietnam has determined that smart and sustainable city development is a breakthrough direction to enhance national competitiveness. Therefore, in the past five years, the government has issued many policies to promote the construction and development of smart cities, such as Decision 950/QD-TTg approving the "project for sustainable smart city development in Vietnam for the period of 2018–2025 and orientation to 2030" and Decision 749/QD-TTg approving the "National Digital Transformation Program to 2025, with an orientation to 2030" (Dangcongsan.vn 2020). As a result of the government's promotion of smart city development, Vietnam ranked 86th in 193 UN member countries in 2020, remaining in the group of 69 countries with a high E-Government Development Index (EGDI) value since 2018, while maintaining a continuous rise from 2014, as stated in the UN's publications (UN E-Government Knowledgebase nd). Currently, nearly 40/63 (63.5%) cities in Vietnam are working with cutting-edge technology to implement smart cities (Lam 2020). However, many current smart city models focus only on technical solutions rather than paying attention to the planning elements, such as maintaining and promoting elements of traditional culture and urban civilization. One of the smart city models in Vietnam that concentrates on planning and encouraging cultural aspects of the city was developed in Thua Thien Hue province, Vietnam.

10.3   Introduction to Thua Thien Hue Province and Its Crucial Concern in Developing a Smart City

The case of the IOC in Thua Thien Hue province is a remarkable example of effective smart city planning and application inside a historical and cultural city in Vietnam. The IOC helps the government supervise and control citizens' social activities and predict social trends. In addition, it encourages two-way communication between the government and citizens/tourists to co-create the city.

The Thua Thien Hue authority understood the high level of complexity in designing and deploying a smart city in their province. First, the extended central city of Thua Thien Hue is large (502,530 km^2) (Thuathienhue.gov.vn nd) and comprises both urban and rural areas. Therefore, different areas of the city are at different levels of development. While some areas already have the necessary infrastructure to develop IOC utilities, access is still limited in others. Another crucial concern for smart city planning is that the rights and participation of all citizens, including the privileged and the marginalized, must be at the center of development. Second, Thua Thien Hue is the cultural and historical center of Vietnam, which has five world heritage sites. The province is committed to sustainable tourism development. However, these sites were in a poor state of preservation due to a lack of cultural heritage supervision, while poor management led to overtourism in peak season. Evidently, tourism is beneficial to Thua Thien Hue province in many ways, but the heavy presence of tourism reduces quality of life for locals. Overtourism could bring about certain social problems, such as damaging fragile environments or landmarks, scaring wildlife, pushing up local rents, and crowding narrow roads (Chan nd). The main objective of the authority is to develop smart city infrastructure inside a cultural city. Accordingly, citizens live in a more comfortable and sustainable environment while tourists enjoy a better cultural travel experience.

However, the authority has managed to complete the IOC project in just 90 days. In order to build the basic technical infrastructure for limited access areas, they collaborated with the biggest telecommunication and technology firm in Vietnam, who possesses the broadest-reaching connectivity infrastructure. They also asked for financial support from the firm. This loan allowed them to deploy smart cities' infrastructure in both urban and rural areas simultaneously (Trung 2019).

As the authority defines the main customers of the province as citizens and visitors, a customer experience approach was applied. The firm collaborating with Thua Thien Hue province authority is a homegrown telecommunication champion who possesses a deep understanding of the consumers in Vietnam. As the firm knows people's preferences by city or area, income level, age group, and gender, the Operations Center was tailored to be responsive to the needs of all citizens and visitors and offered integrated services across several functional areas such as transport, security, and collaborative government. The IOC is applied in 7/9 districts (77.8%) and in 100% of specialized organizations under the province's central authority. Camera sensors are installed around the province, especially inside and outside the historical sites for the purpose of supervising. Traffic, public order, and security are closely regulated. As a result, Thua Thien Hue province's cultural sites are protected, which allows the province to deliver a better travel experience for tourists. The IOC project of Thua Thien Hue province won the prize for "most innovative smart city project" in Asia in the Telecom Asia Awards 2019 (Thua Thien Hue IOC 2019a, b, c, d, e, f, g, h). The next part of this paper will shed light on how the authority can develop an intangible smart city infrastructure while preserving cultural and historical values in Thua Thien Hue.

10.4 The Intelligent Operations Center

The IOC in Thua Thien Hue was launched in 2019 and has contributed to the city in many ways. First, by handling, supervising, coordinating, and controlling data, the center not only helps strengthen management capability but also reduces the cost of government maintenance. The problems the center has addressed are described below:

- The Operations Center currently allows residents and companies to fill 2300 administrative forms online, which saves time and effort for both residents and government officials.
- The IOC solves management problems that require timely information about every aspect of the city functioning by making resources readily available. The authority can thus make immediate and reasonable policy decisions.
- The public administration supervision service solution addresses problems caused by humans such as government officials' bureaucratic and systematic errors. By June 2019, the system had identified 41,764 violations, including 10,268 at the provincial level (25%), 21,675 at the district level (52%) and 9821 (23%) at the communal level. Time-consuming and cumbersome administrative work is transformed into a fast and easy process (Thua Thien Hue IOC 2019a, b, c, d, e, f, g, h).
- The smart card for government officials helps track the presence of officials more easily to avoid potential fraud (Thua Thien Hue IOC 2019a, b, c, d, e, f, g, h).
- The IOC also offers journalism and media management. The system automatically verifies 98.25% of news and feedback relating to Thua Thien Hue province. The authority can thus make timely decisions to handle each case. A mere 1.75% of the news items need to be sent to organizations for observation. Using machine learning, the system scans and collects all online information related to Thua Thien Hue province from all sources such as websites, Facebook, and blogs. Collected data is then automatically analyzed by the system, which labels the nuances of

the news (negative news, positive news, etc.) and other management information. In the first phase, the IOC will re-verify and distribute the information to relevant specialized agencies depending on the content of the news. If sensitive or fake news is collected, the scenario "information crisis" will be activated according to the regulations and operating procedures of Thua Thien Hue province. In the first six months of 2019, the system identified around 1100 news items about Thua Thien Hue scanned from 1 million electronic newspapers, 40 million Facebook accounts, and 150 thousand Facebook groups and fan pages, with 731 (66%) positive news, 197 negative news (18.2%), and 171 fake news (15.8%) (Thua Thien Hue IOC 2019a, b, c, d, e, f, g, h). By tracking and categorizing citizens' and tourists' feedback on the internet, the authority can understand their needs and thus design better living and travel experiences.

Second, the IOC helps to promote urban safety. Camera sensors are installed around the province, especially inside and outside the historical sites for the purpose of supervising. These 200 cameras apply face recognition and crowd recognition to ensure urban security and regulate traffic. Urban order is ensured by detecting encroachments on sidewalks and illegal parking; traffic is regulated by counting and capturing the license plates of vehicles that commit traffic violations. Also, the IOC observes the entire city with a bird's eye view. Specifically, using an artificial intelligence solution, the system will analyze and issue warnings of violation and provide the appropriate processing time: instantaneous or in a certain period (Thua Thien Hue IOC 2019a, b, c, d, e, f, g, h). Cold penalties will be given in case of traffic violations, urban order violations, and environmental sanitation violations. As a result, Thua Thien Hue province in general and its cultural sites in particular are protected, which allows the province to deliver a better travel experience for tourists and better living conditions for its residents.

Third, all IT security issues are closely controlled by the latest applications. Information safety supervision for the LAN[1]/WAN[2] system, data center, server, email system, and general/shared applications is offered 24/7 by IT experts. The center uses four of the latest applications, namely Centralized Virus and Internet Attack Prevention, Web Application Firewall, Intended Attack Detection, and Centralized Security Supervision. The center provides real-time information safety warnings by displaying the source of attacks on the system and the targets that are being attacked. At the same time, it provides security analysis to give effective solutions for protecting and preventing security attacks (Thua Thien Hue IOC 2019a, b, c, d, e, f, g, h).

Fourth, citizen and tourist relationships and satisfaction are better managed using an application called Hue-S. Leaders of the People's Committee of Thua Thien Hue Province consider citizens and tourists as central to their mission and operations, so by launching the Hue-S application, a part of IOC, they are beginning to develop a stronger bond with their residents and visitors. Basically, the Hue-S application

---

[1] A LAN (local area network) is a group of connected computers and network devices, usually within the same building.

[2] A WAN (wide area network) connects several LANs and may be limited to an enterprise (a corporation or an organization) or accessible to the public.

acts as a real-time contact point between residents/tourists and the local authorities. The application receives all complaints about municipal issues from citizens and visitors in the province. This feature of the Hue-S application also helps residents and visitors to monitor, interact with, and evaluate the level of satisfaction with the results of each agency's handling. The application allows for quicker and easier access to non-emergency municipal services and information, as well as improving the effectiveness and efficiency of governmental services. Use of the Hue-S application has resulted in a sound base for improving the satisfaction and cooperation of citizens and tourists with the local authorities. Considering the large increase in the number of requests received and handled recently, governmental services have improved. By March 2021, more than 350,000 people in the area installed and used the Hue-S application, accounting for nearly 50% of the province's smartphone users. All the specialized organizations under the People's Committee of Thua Thien Hue Province and 7/9 (77.8%) of the People's Committee of Districts have applied to the IOC to receive incident reports and handle incidents. In the first six months in 2019, the Hue-S application received 1400 responses and successfully sanctioned 80 related infringing agencies. The respondents were mostly satisfied with the way results were handled: 67.6% of respondents were satisfied with the handling results, 21.8% accepted the handling results and only 10.6% were not satisfied. Because they are co-creators of the smart city project, people are more willing to share their information. They believe the risk of losing privacy does not outweigh the potential benefits of a smart city (Thua Thien Hue IOC 2019a, b, c, d, e, f, g, h).

In addition, a variety of different communication channels is important to reach a broad range of citizens and tourists. All official alerts about criminals, frequent fraud, fake news, counterfeit goods, traffic jams, accidents, dangerous weather, natural disasters, and epidemics are immediately communicated through the application. In November 2020, through the warning function, 50,000 users of Hue-S in Thua Thien Hue received notifications about storms No. 5 and 13, including updates on the progress of storms, tropical depression, natural disasters, or electricity safety warnings in case of storms. These warnings appear immediately on the notification screens of their smartphones, helping people access accurate and timely information in difficult communication conditions (Dinh 2020). As a result, people can actively respond to natural disasters, minimizing loss of life and property damage.

In addition to providing emergency warnings and updates, the Hue-S application allows tourists to discover many interesting cultural and historical places and events as well as good local restaurants. The application helps to push the benefits of the tourism economy toward less crowded urban areas by exposing tourists to other underrated travel destinations and activities in the provinces. Also, this exposure limits pressure on the most popular tourist attractions and restaurants. Accordingly, tourist attractions in the central area can offer better tourism services, while the quality of life for locals in these areas is ensured.

Fifth, the IOC solves environment supervision problems. Environmental sensors are installed in densely populated areas, industrial zones, lakes, and dams as well as areas where floods frequently occur. The software system synthesizes data from the sensors, analyzes environmental pollution, air, and water environments, then integrates the environmental management data of Phu Bai Industrial Zone with the center to save time. Additionally, the center inspects dams and regulates traffic for areas with frequent floods during the rainy season. During this season, the system also provides residents with images directly through Hue-S applications (Thua Thien Hue IOC 2019a, b, c, d, e, f, g, h).

Sixth, the IOC offers fishing vessel monitoring solutions. The center helps monitor fishing vessels on the sea and records fishing vessels' voyages. Its main functions are giving automatic warnings when a fishing vessel goes out of the Vietnamese territorial sea, receiving SOS signals from fishing vessels, and sending storm warning signals. The center has installed equipment on fishing vessels and is now conducting monitoring, testing, and evaluating the effectiveness of the solution (Thua Thien Hue IOC 2019a, b, c, d, e, f, g, h).

10.5 Conclusion and Recommendations

As can be seen from the features of the IOC described here, Thua Thien Hue's local authority has worked with smart city initiatives to develop smart city infrastructure, focusing on enhancing the living experience of residents and the travel experience of tourists. They consider technology as an instrument to help design the center rather than as a focus. Accordingly, citizens and visitors in Thua Thien Hue province work as valued co-creators of the smart city project. The authority thus has successfully provided sustainable living conditions for its inhabitants, managed tourism effectively, and protected the province's historical sites and cultural values.

The future of urban tourism belongs to smart cities. To boost tourism and increase the participation of inhabitants in co-creating more value for the province in the smart city project, this paper makes the following recommendations about conducting sustainable marketing campaigns for the center.

(1) The authority is now using Hue-S to introduce new tourist attractions to visitors. However, to turn awareness about attractions into action, the authority should create and encourage the use of travel cards integrated with the Hue-S application to stimulate tourist flows to less crowded tourist attractions. A Hop-On, Hop-Off[3] bus tour is a good idea to show tourists the targeted destinations. At the same time, developers should create 3D maps for these destinations on the application to attract tourists. Moreover, Hue-S should operate as a social platform where users can become content creators to promote information-sharing behavior. The authority should give incentives to people who share their travel experiences and make it easy for them to give reviews about tourist destinations and events on Hue-S.

---

[3] Hop-On, Hop-Off or HOHO buses follow a specific route with stops close to major city attractions. Commuters can board the bus from any of the designated stops, hop off at the attraction they want to visit, and simply hop back on the next bus when they want to continue.

(2) Additionally, to promote responsible behaviors in inhabitants, the local administration of Hue-S can create interactive games and quizzes about "how to be a responsible tourist and citizen" or "how to protect cultural heritage sites." These games and quizzes will promote responsible attitudes among visitors and residents. These activities will also help spread awareness and publicize the preservation of the area's heritage

References

Bettencourt LA (1997) Customer voluntary performance: customers as partners in service delivery. J Retail 73(3):383–406

European Commission (nd) Smart cities. https://ec.europa.eu/info/eu-regional-and-urban-development/topics/cities-and-urban-development/city-initiatives/smart-cities_en. Accessed 11 Apr 2021

Dameri RP (2013) Searching for smart city definition: a comprehensive proposal. Int J Comput Technol 11(5):2544–2551

Dangcongsan.vn (nd) Hội nghị cấp cao thành phố thông minh Việt Nam 2020. https://dangcongsan.vn/khoa-giao/hoi-nghi-cap-cao-thanh-pho-thong-minh-viet-nam-2020-568518.html. Accessed 11 Apr 2021

Dinh V (2020) Thừa Thiên - Huế: Chủ động ứng phó với bão số 13. https://baotainguyenmoitruong.vn/thua-thien-hue-chu-dong-ung-pho-voi-bao-so-13-315688.html. Accessed 11 Apr 2021

Dong B et al (2008) The effects of customer participation in co-created service recovery. J Acad Mark Sci 36(1):123–137

Ennew CT, Binks MR (1999) Impact of participative service relationships on quality, satisfaction and retention: an exploratory study. J Bus Res 46(2):121–132

Harvard T.H. Chan School of Public Health (nd) The problem of 'overtourism.' https://www.hsph.harvard.edu/news/hsph-in-the-news/the-problem-of-overtourism/. Accessed 11 Apr 2021

Hsieh YC et al (2018) Does raising value co-creation increase all customers' happiness? J Bus Ethics 152(4):1053–1067

Journal of Building Materials (2020) "Phát triển thành phố thông minh tại Việt Nam" 9/2020 (electronic service)

Lam T (2020) Phát triển đô thị thông minh là chuyển đổi số cho đô thị https://nhandan.com.vn/thong-tin-so/phat-trien-do-thi-thong-minh-la-chuyen-doi-so-cho-do-thi-625579/. Accessed 11 Apr 2021

Nexusintegra (nd) Top 10 smart cities. https://nexusintegra.io/top-10-smart-cities/. Accessed 11 Apr 2021

Nguyen H (2019) Thành phố thông minh: Xu hướng phát triển trên thế giới và Việt Nam, Tạp chí Kiến Trúc. https://www.tapchikientruc.com.vn/chuyen-muc/thanh-pho-thong-minh-xu-huong-phat-trien-tren-the-gioi-va-viet-nam.html. Accessed 11 Apr 2021

Ragatz GL et al (2002) Benefits associated with supplier integration into new product development under conditions of technology uncertainty. J Bus Res 55(5):389–400

Thua Thien Hue IOC (2019a, June 28) Giải pháp giám sát dịch vụ hành chính công. https://ioc.thuathienhue.gov.vn/?gd=29&cn=672&tc=821. Accessed 11 Apr 2021

Thua Thien Hue IOC (2019b, June 28). Giải pháp thẻ điện tử. https://ioc.thuathienhue.gov.vn/?gd=29&cn=672&tc=816. Accessed 11 Apr 2021

Thua Thien Hue IOC (2019c, June 28) Giải pháp giám sát thông tin báo chí. https://ioc.thuathienhue.gov.vn/?gd=29&cn=672&tc=822. Accessed 11 Apr 2021

Thua Thien Hue IOC (2019d, June 28) Giải pháp giám sát đô thị thông qua cảm biến camera. https://ioc.thuathienhue.gov.vn/?gd=29&cn=672&tc=824. Accessed 11 Apr 2021

Thua Thien Hue IOC (2019e, June 28) Giải pháp giám sát đảm bảo an toàn thông tin. https://ioc.
    thuathienhue.gov.vn/?gd=29&cn=672&tc=817. Accessed 11 Apr 2021
Thua Thien Hue IOC (2019g, June 28) Giải pháp giám sát môi trường. https://ioc.thuathienhue.gov.
    vn/?gd=29&cn=672&tc=818. Accessed 11 Apr 2021
Thua Thien Hue IOC (2019h, June 28) Giải pháp giám sát tàu cá. https://ioc.thuathienhue.gov.vn/?
    gd=29&cn=672&tc=815. Accessed 11 Apr 2021
Thua Thien Hue IOC (2021) Trung tâm Giám sát, điều hành đô thị thông minh. https://ioc.thuath
    ienhue.gov.vn. Accessed 11 Apr 2021
Thua Thien Hue IOC (2019f, June 28) Giải pháp phản ánh hiện trường. https://ioc.thuathienhue.
    gov.vn/?gd=29&cn=672&tc=823. Accessed 11 Apr 2021
Thuathienhue.gov.vn (nd) Geographical position and natural features: general introduction. https://
    thuathienhue.gov.vn/en-us/Home/Detail/tid/General-introduction/newsid/B6EF830D-A48B-
    42F7-A1A6-A9990110B5F1/cid/D6E7F610-5757-467E-B384-94E7458D4286. Accessed 11
    Apr 2021
Trung P (2019) Giải sáng tạo châu Á: Thành phố thông minh Thừa Thiên—Huế với những
    điều đặc biệt. https://nhandan.vn/thong-tin-so/giai-sang-tao-chau-a-thanh-pho-thong-minh-thua-
    thien-hue-voi-nhung-dieu-dac-biet-359697/. Accessed 11 Apr 2021
UN E-Government Knowledgebase (nd) E-government development index. https://publicadministr
    ation.un.org/egovkb/en-us/Data/Country-Information/id/189-Viet-Nam. Accessed 11 Apr 2021
Yi Y et al (2011) Customer participation and citizenship behavioral influences on employee
    performance, satisfaction, commitment, and turnover intention. J Bus Res 64(1):87–95